Rules & Religion:

Wrecking America

**Why churches & the Government can't solve
our problems!**

By Benjamin D. Goss, MBA

: Butterfly Promotions, LLC | © 2012 Omaha, NE;
© 2015 revised

ISBN 9780996183505
Library of Congress Cataloguing-in-Publication Data
(Registration is pending)

DEDICATION

To my lovely wife Jenna, and my very active & amazing children, thank you for your love and support of my many efforts.

Thank you to Shane Borza, Jenna (Prather) Goss, and Thor Knutstad for your time and thoughtful comments that have helped to shape the outcome of this book. Thank you Mom & Dad for important life lessons, for your support and your love.

Thank you to the thousands of dedicated patriots from every walk of life, including members of the Constitution Party, there are many who struggle each day to have our country return to its Constitutionally-bounded roots.

Thank you to our everyday American heroes that lay their lives on the line, including the ultimate sacrifice at times, whether they are our local, state and federal law enforcement agents, firefighters, and our men and women in uniform – your defense of our freedoms and your efforts to safeguard our lives – make it possible for us to enjoy freedom unprecedented in the world, even today.

Table of Contents

Chapter One:
Where Do We Begin?

"In matters of style, swim with the current;
in matters of principle, stand like a rock ...
~Thomas Jefferson

I predict future happiness for Americans if they can prevent the
government from wasting the labors of the people under the pretense
of taking care of them."
~Thomas Jefferson

     http://www.benjamingoss.com

In 1882, Mark Twain wrote, "Reader, suppose you were an idiot. And suppose you were a member of Congress. But I repeat myself." In that same line of thought, I submit to you that anyone who thinks that religion and state can be truly separate is an idiot. The dictionary defines an idiot as a "person so mentally deficient as to be incapable of ordinary reasoning," and secondly as "an utterly foolish or senseless person." Why?

It is very simple: everyone, without exception, operates based on personal faith. Whoever came up with the idea that the separation of church and state is somehow synonymous with the utter prevention of anyone involving their faith in how they express themselves and how they make decisions is an idiot! When the founders of our country framed the Constitution and the subsequent Bill of Rights, they created "freedom of religion" and the expression thereof to avoid the abusive tyranny of one religion holding sway over all others. The amendment was not written as freedom FROM religion.

At its heart, the framers were trying to avoid the results of religious tyranny that stripped Catholics, Huguenots, Protestants, Puritans, Muslims and Jews alike of their rights to life, liberty and property during the 15th, 16th, and 17th Centuries in various parts of the world. John Locke articulately presented this political thought in the 16th Century. Preventing the loss of property and preventing religious persecution was the intent, it was not designed to prevent the practice or expression of faith.

This work is a call to the American principles of Freedom; it is *not* *a call to religious patriotism*. It is vitally important that you grasp the context for this work. Without understanding the perspective of the precepts on which this work is based, then nothing useful can come from the conversation.

First, if you are looking for references to the Bible, scriptures, or some other Holy Writ, that is neither the purpose nor the design for this conversation. Should you so choose, I am confident you will be able to discern the intrinsic value of each point as you consider it.

Second, the word "church" is used generically throughout as a reference to religious organizations, and is not specifically meant to refer to Christianity. Whether you visit an ashram, a synagogue, a mosque, or what many people refer to as "church," please consider the use of the word to be representative thereof. It is simply a shorter way of referring collectively to the numerous types of religious organizations and institutions that exist today.

Third, the use of the word government, small "g" is purposefully different from the use of the word Government, big "G." Small "g" is used in reference to the concepts of governance, and how we as a people, or nation, choose to govern ourselves. Big "G" specifically refers to the Federal Government of the United States, as well as the perspective that many people have of the Government as an entity as opposed to the tool or the process that we call government or governance.

Fourth, this work builds on the concept that truths and principles are both foundational and interrelated. Our laws are not written with the idea that truth and facts are variable. However, there are many who think that we, as a nation, can live with a relative sense of right and wrong. The application of law demonstrates that it is neither practical nor reasonable to operate on such a sliding and slippery scale.

Fifth, the overriding and dominant political theology in operation is Secular Humanism. While there are certainly those who are not Secular Humanists, the philosophy is now predominant. In fact, it has so invaded our socio-political thought that many who practice a faith now awkwardly and inappropriately find themselves verbally assaulted in public for making faith-based statements. Even statements generically understood as family values are debased. This has become so pervasive that even a comment made by a private individual, such as Dan Cathy, CEO of Chik-Fil-A, finds himself and his company attacked for asserting that faith in public (circa July 2012).

A leading tenant of Secular Humanism is that truth can be found through the dialectic process, in essence the belief that there should be discussion resolving in consensus. Perhaps you remember the following from high school science or philosophy. Thesis and Antithesis collide, synthesize, and create a new Thesis. It sounds so reasonable does it not? The practical realities of law and justice, however, do not allow for this movable scale of truth and justice or right and wrong.

Sixth, this work is a conversation that seeks to discuss concepts that can be known and understood as true. Truth is not subject to whims that blow continually adjusting to societal definitions of what is and is not "real" or "true." The (*Hegelian*) dialectic process, which is Greek and western in origin, simply cannot carry the weight of conversation nor does it bear up under the requirements of law because of its varying nature. [1]

Seventh, this work submits that the current loud and often vitriolic conversation, about whether we should "Return to the Faith of Our Fathers" or if we should rely on Government to legislate the solutions to all that ails us, is insufficient. The conversation on both sides is most often framed as being which "G" should we, or do we want to listen to, God or Government. This is *"THE WRONG CONVERSATION!"* If we ask Government to "deliver both Freedom and Virtue it will give us neither".[2] The same can be said for Religion. Thus, we come to a brief understanding of the century old conflict over the meaning of the Establishment Clause.

This clause is taken from the First Amendment in the Bill of Rights, appending the United States Constitution, where our founders wrote, "Congress shall make no law respecting an establishment of religion." Most everyone would agree that Government should not

---

[1] Dr. Marlene McMillan, Why Liberty Matters, whylibertymatters.com, personal interview, ~06.2010

[2] Kevin Miller, Vanguard Institute, Values Aligned Leadership Summit, 04.2010

be dictating virtue. While churches would seemingly be the forum for discussions regarding virtue, the tendency for most churches is an autocratic and dictatorial bent to this conversation. In the end, most churches seek to legislate their beliefs regarding virtue rather than remain focused on the development of virtue in community, one heart at a time.

Eighth, the thought process behind this work is an attempt to utilize truths that we can see in nature and the experiences of life, specifically those experiences with the nature of groups. The reality is that we find healthy community in the concept of "organism." Whereas an understanding of our fragmented view of society is that, the end result is that of "organization." It is important to understand that the church (small "c" as an organization) is not the same thing as the Universal Church (a theological concept). It is also important to understand the difference between government and Government in terms of philosophy, utility and expression. This is the overarching contrast framing our discussion throughout.

Ninth, our western mindset has created a continually fragmenting and broken perspective that one's faith can be separated from how one governs, or perhaps more generically, from how one makes decisions. If we consider nature, then we reconnect to truth and begin to grasp the interconnectedness of things. We cannot expect someone to divorce their value system from their decision matrix and way of thought, any more than we can expect pollution seeping into a river to avoid killing plants and fish downstream.

Yet there are those who scream against even moderate expressions of faith on the basis that it somehow violates the "establishment clause" regarding religion. It is unnatural, unhealthy, and utterly foolish. The "Religion-Free" Government types are actually saying that Secular Humanism (SH) is the rightful religion of the land. How can I say that? Because SH is just as religious in tone, flavor and fervor as any adherent of Christianity or Islam. Despite their defiant, dissonant and loud protests against this idea, it is absolutely true. Instead of being honest about the reality of their views, they instead climb upon altars of condescension dripping with the oil of their disdain decrying those of other faiths.

Their position holds that their religious persuasion, SH, finds the expression of any faith (usually and frequently the Christian faith) to be abhorrent to their mind. Thus, we find ourselves in the midst of a torrid onslaught of secular humanism parading itself as not religious, when in reality it presents a specific set of values and precepts on which its proponents have placed their faith.

Tenth, the strength of the western mindset is the ability to separate a whole into its various parts. As a result, we have an excellent opportunity to examine various aspects of faith, logic, and disparate points of view. It provides us with a quality micro-perspective that gives understanding. Where it falters is when that systematic examination seeks to place the parts back within the context of a system. For in most cases, the parts are left "on the cutting room floor," and never reassembled to understand how they fit together as a whole. The macro-perspective is sadly missing.

For too long, we have allowed Liberal-Big-Government proponents (LBGs) to dictate the lines of battle and to define the language with which it is fought. Virtue Politics is *NOT* the battleground. The battleground has always been *Freedom*; unfortunately, most of us have walked away from this fight. *Why?* I believe that it is because conjoined with freedom is personal responsibility. Freedom cannot exist without individuals taking responsibility to preserve, protect, guide and then pass it along to the next generation.

Eleventh, we as Americans generically, and churches specifically, have surrendered our personal and corporate responsibility to care for our fellow man and set the standard for a virtuous society. As a result, the secular humanist has aggressively invaded Government and even now seeks to criminalize virtues that they abhor, and criminalize the lack of adherence to values and ideals they hold dear (e.g. homosexuality, fatty foods, soda, and health care). For too long we have allowed Government to confuse virtue with freedom. The new definition equals the Tyranny we declared independence from so many years ago! Virtue ought to be the realm of the community as discussed with our pastors and lived out in freedom, not determined by our Government and sidestepped by our pastors.

Twelfth, this collection of essays transparently seeks to discuss how so many churches have walked away from their responsibility to properly build community. Instead, too many churches seek to propagate their disparate and separate institutions. It also seeks to demonstrate that Government is overstepping its bounds by seeking to institute virtue when it cannot and should not be anything more than an organization limited in influence and restrained in scope. The sad truth is that our churches are becoming more politically organized and our politics are becoming more and more religious-ized. In the past, church leaders commented on politics, but were not in and of themselves political. Our Government, as founded, was originally designed as a guarantee against the abuse of power, rather than the assertion of controls over issues, which rightfully ought to remain the domain of one's private life, local community, and state.

The last thought for your consideration is that at some point all illustrations break down. Why? Because they are only meant to aid in understanding, and they are not meant to completely define a concept or principle in its entirety with exacting precision. Whether you are reading this to better understand how to "heart check" the moving parts of a church, or because you want to prod dialogue about the appropriate role of government, the purpose of these essays is to prod your heart, stimulate your mind and create a positive forum for understanding. I seek to create a basis for reasonable conversation. Alas, sane dialogue is something that is sorely lacking in our world today, but especially in the halls of American polity and religion.

Chapter Two:
How they deal with public assistance

*"A government big enough to give you everything you want
is a government big enough to take from you everything you have…"*
~President Gerald R. Ford; To Congress; 12 August 1974.

In this complex world, one of the most trying issues at hand, overwhelmingly typical of third world countries, is a severe lack of resources. Those resources include everything from the monumental; food, water, and transportation; to the mundane, footwear, clothes, and books. Truly, this is a powerfully pivotal matter. Consequently, it is also one that is the crux of political maneuvering and blather. Countering this ineptitude, it is also an area where many non-profit organizations, usually faith-based groups, have a tendency to excel. However, it is an area where they fail brilliantly as well.

For example, you may or may not be aware that after the Hurricane Katrina disaster that approximately 15 base camps were set up as distribution centers to aid those in need. Of these base camps, only one was run by Christian non-profit organizations. The other 14 were operated by the Federal Government, specifically the Federal Emergency Management Agency (FEMA). A little known fact, little known as it defies the logic of the liberal media, is the truth that the one non-profit base distributed more goods and services to the needy of Louisiana than the other 14 FEMA-operated bases combined. If you would like to read more about this, The Institute for Homeland Security Solutions published a report that generalized findings from a variety of sources regarding "Faith-Based and Community Organizations' Participation in Emergency Preparedness and Response Activities" (February 2010). For another look at this, read the last section of the report provided regarding lessons learned by the George W. Bush Whitehouse (http://georgewbush-whitehouse.archives.gov/reports/katrina-lessons-learned/chapter5.html).

What does this prove? One sole instance does not prove anything. However, there are many examples of government inefficiency that, as a whole, prove that Government is not an appropriate channel for the distribution of goods and services. When we as Americans abdicated our hearts to the institution of the Government, we excised our hearts from the process. Even so, according to the Giving USA Foundation, Americans have given an average of 4% to charities over the past four decades. In comparison to the socialist countries of Europe, Americans have out-given their European counterparts by a factor of more than 10 to 1. While many would consider 4% to be a horrendously low number, it exceeds the resources offered up by many of world's economies.

Nevertheless, churches today face many of the same problems that we find in Government. Churches, largely, have become institutions that require support, and in many instances what we find is that individuals give to the organization and expect that institution, whatever its form or expression as a non-profit, Para-church, or church organization, should produce a "return-on-donation (ROD)" otherwise known as a "return-on-investment" (ROI).

What is the difference between this and the absentee parent that floods their child with lavish gifts out of an over-wrought sense of guilt for not being present? There is no difference.

Organisms Nurture

Organisms by their nature must nurture resources in order to ensure that there will be enough for them to use both now and in the future. Consider your body; it provides resources to every part of your extremities in the appropriate amounts as needed in order to meet the demands of your environment. This is a nurturing aspect of dealing with resources.

Churches encourage individuals to give generously so that they can turn around and mete those resources out to those in need. However, they also require that the mechanism of the church (organization) receive resources in order to sustain itself. An organization, by its nature is not self-sustaining and requires its membership, or "extremities," to provide the resources to function. The result is a lessening of resources for the larger community within which that church-organization operates.

When we surrender our hearts by giving to institutions, then we are separated from the blessing of giving. As a result, instead of being nurturing with resources, our resources behave more as a body does when it enters hypothermia. The limbs become cold, and they threaten to die due to a lack of sufficient blood flow as their connection with the rest of the body is reduced. At the very least, our own hearts are in danger of dying as we separate ourselves from the point of giving. Within the act of giving itself, there is a super charge to the heart where one's entire being is energized by simple effort made in helping another member of the community. That occurs regardless of the expression of one's faith, which no one should or ought to deny.

Government, by its nature, cannot be nurturing. It was never designed to be nurturing. Thus, when people expect the Government to provide that kind of societal care, what they are actually given is inept, poorly constructed, ill-advised and incompetent use of resources. This is demonstrated by rampant fraud, ridiculous delays and wait times, and a general malaise on the spirit of those forced to participate therewith.

Organizations Compete

Here is the heart check for the group that seeks to demonstrate its willingness to get outside the typical box. The number one problem with any group, organization, enterprise, or church is that there is a tendency to operate from a perspective of the lack of resources, or out of the seeming desperation of need. Not on the part of those in need, but on the part of those who have the resources to lend. This overly strong drive of need creates a competitive atmosphere where budgets are justified, an ROI is defined, and we attempt to measure or marginalize the needs of those who require resources. Why is this?

Need is an undeniable driver in the midst of organizational resource management, and it says:

- There is not enough to go around so we have to be careful with what we have.

- Due to limited resources, we cannot respond to need, we can only respond to a verified, or verifiable, assessment of necessity.

- Change the focus from being the individual, or family, in need, and place it on the organization's need to generate a "positive ROI" in their giving a.k.a. resource management.

- That when raising money, or gathering it, we tell stories about what we do, but there is no real connection between the donor and the recipient.

- That "Needs" compete for resources because they are of necessity and in reality limited.

The unfortunate truth is that neither Government nor churches seem to realize in their institutionalized wisdom and in their methodical processes, that their very drive for efficiency creates inefficiency. They have consistently failed to see that their focus turns toward the application of resources at hand, rather than a focus on the need at hand.

The competition for resources is not just competition for the money, or whatever forms the resource takes. It is competition for attention. Competition for the one in need to justify that their need is more important than the needs of others that may also be under consideration.

The result of Government taking over providing a helping hand has resulted in churches, apparently willingly, abdicating their traditional role in this area with the false assumption that somehow Government is more capable to meet the needs of people by meting out limited resources. The cold hard reality is that if Government would get out of the way and return billions of dollars in wasted resources, then there would be an abundance of resources to churches, non-profits and the like. As money flows back into the hands and hearts of the people that generate that value, their ability to exercise their hearts in charity would benefit this country, and the world over, like no other time in recorded history!

An organic perspective of resources enables us to see that the concept of scarcity is false. Instead, we must embrace the reality is that there is an abundance of resources in the world today. We must come to understand that the global struggle is distribution, not the presence or production of resources. Perhaps it would be better if we phrase it as follows; "challenges exist in moving resources from the point of creation to the point of need." It is counterproductive and foolishly alarmist to feed into the hysteria of a modern LBG media that screams about lack of resources. The LBG alarmist seeks only to produce fear because fear allows them to exert control over public opinion. Fear and scarcity are frequently used to promote agendas that are neither sane, nor reasonable, nor reflective of the true nature of things.

Instead, we ought to operate with the understanding that resources are sufficient to the needs that present themselves. The question remains, are we able to communicate with the heart effectively so that those resources will be released in due time? Or, will we excise the heart, remove resources from the body and abandon the application of those resources to some remote entity that lacks first-hand knowledge of the need for which it has been tasked to meet? The body should be considered as synonymous with those who make up the citizens or members of any community, large or small.

Unfortunately, many churches and non-profits fall into the same trap that is found in the Government's abusive waste of taxpayer dollars. They outsource and place in committee the expressed needs of those who simply need their needs met. In April of 2010, in a case of the "Good-Samaritan-Who-Wasn't" a homeless man was stabbed to death on a street, and passersby simply let him die. Moreover, it was all caught on videotape! The apathy of institutionalized giving and charity has transcended the halls of micromanagement to dull the hearts and minds of the average citizen. Thus, churches have sadly become increasingly like government, and as a result ***both*** are equally and wrenchingly ineffective.

Chapter Three:
How they progress

*"The natural progress of things is for liberty to yield,
and government to gain ground."*
~President Thomas Jefferson

Does anyone in his or her right - or left - mind even know what progress should be? What should it look like? There are the "progressives" who would have us think that socializing our system of life, from medicine, to government, to financial institutions, to how our country creates value is the "modern" – and therefore best – way to go. But what does progress really mean?

I appreciate the proverbial saying "If pro is the opposite of con, what is the opposite of progress?" Answer: "Congress!" Perhaps another way to consider that thought is this: if you want to ruin something, then just involve a committee.

Is it not true that committees can produce positive benefits? The reality is that a committee, depending on its makeup, will run one of several distinct paths: 1) rubberstamp of the most powerful opinion; 2) create meaningful "dialogue" about the "preferred" direction; or 3) make decisions based on the merits of the arguments. The problem with most committees, however, is that rather than relying on the concept of truth, they crumble in on options one and two. Certainly, other options can be suggested, but the reality is that committees are frequently problematic and cursed with the vagaries of every seedy aspect of group dynamics *(a.k.a. politics)* as well as the positives.

At the end of the day, the true benefit of committees and legislative bodies in governance is the ability, when properly wielded, to protect disparate groups from savaging each other. Progress happens when organizations make themselves small and get out of the way.

Is a church an organization or an organism? Yes. However, how an individual church organization chooses to rule itself and express itself will determine whether or not the *organic* aspects of church community will win through the trappings of organization.

How do churches measure, or establish progress? Many churches use numbers to justify their existence. For example, I can recall one particular ministry talking about the "numbers" or statistics of what they "produced." They said, we had "5,000 conversions just last year alone." But what does that number truly reflect? What is the follow through? Are those folks plugged into communities where they can learn, grow and flourish in their newly found faith? Or, do many walk away from their newfound faith because they cannot find anyone who is willing or able to help them understand how it connects with their life!

Organisms Grow

When considering the nature of an organism in its proper setting, we see evidence all around us. Organisms grow. They are not stagnant. They are vibrant. They exist in the midst of complex relationships that run the gamut from parasitic to symbiotic. When we take time to consider the context of life, we should realize that we are not just independent we are also interdependent. Most people agree with the saying that "no man is an island."

On the flipside however, one might argue that any one man (or woman) can be an island, it is just that people have a tendency to come and go to and from their island A LOT. Therefore, even those of us that operate somewhat independently of others, still need to visit the mainland and receive visitors.

Organisms begin small and they grow larger. As they grow larger, they become more complex and they require more support to continue to subsist. One might argue that at some level all things reach a level of maximum growth. However, the reality is that, while as individuals we cease to physically grow we do not stop growing in knowledge and experience. Properly applied we ought to become wise. As we move out into our surrounding environments, we continually expand our personal context, and thus we continue to grow.

If we cease to grow, we begin to die.

Community is the ultimate organism. It is an expression of organisms that have self-organized into a larger group with others who are similarly aligned. While the nature of an organism is to grow, develop, and mature, the same cannot be said for an organization. Government, as organization, can and will flex as needed, but it should not step outside its designed box.

Yet, that is what we expect of our churches. For some vague and ill-defined, or simply ignored, reason the organizational aspects of our churches are allowed to stand in the way of the natural and organic nature of faith communities. As a result, we kill the heart of what should have been our "organic community of faith" and replaced it with a heartless shadow of what could have been.

Disheartening, dissatisfying, disastrous and deconstructionist...

Organizations Restrain

The nature of organizations is the concept of restraint. John Locke's concept of social contract theory speaks quite eloquently to this thought:

When Locke comes to explain how government comes into being, he uses the idea that people agree that their condition in the state of nature is unsatisfactory, and so agree to transfer some of their rights to a central government, while retaining others. This is the theory of the social contract ... *"any civil government depends on the consent of those who are governed, which may be withdrawn at any time."* (http://plato.stanford.edu/entries/locke/).

In other words, we relinquish limited rights in order to enjoy a greater expression of other rights. Freedom is found in limited restraint that allows greater expression. It is within the kernels of these thoughts that the concepts of the rights to life, liberty and property are guaranteed. While American civil government practitioners were theorists at the time of the writing of the Declaration of Independence, they wrote about the inherent right of every human being to experience life, liberty and the pursuit of happiness.

The purpose of government then, is organizational and not organic. Yet, what do we see? There has been an unabridged history of more than 100 years of continued rapacious growth in American Federal Government. This growth is demonstrated by an avaricious appetite consuming all it touches, and unfortunately at this point in time without restraint. When government lacks restraint, it demonstrates aspects of being an organism that are both unnatural and unhealthy for the communities it was designed to protect. The government consumes resources in terms of manpower, in terms of currency (a.k.a. value), in terms of rights - a continuing encroachment against the freedoms we used to enjoy - and in terms of Constitutional guarantees to local governance, rather than the overpowering Federal governance we now enjoy.

And so we are faced with a stark choice; are we going to continue to stomach this upside down and crazy world, which is attempting to force us to agree that the roles of both organisms and organizations should be changed? Do we want our government to be more like church and for our churches to be more like government? NO! The system as it currently runs amuck is categorically failing!

Government needs to cease its growth and return to the box that was designed for it. Churches need to step outside the false security of "well run organizations" and fall upon the heart of what they were meant to be: communities growing and developing in a mature support of the individual parts.

Someone once commented to me on Facebook, "Why should I care what 50 old white farts decided to do 250 years ago?" At first, I was taken aback, and then I realized the proper response ... three days later! That is how we are supposed to learn correct? When an apparent truth is challenged, we need to critically consider what the challenge means, and whether or not the context of that truth has been properly assessed.

When faced with that question, the appropriate response is that *"there is nothing new under the sun."* We need to stop making the false and ill-considered thought that technology creates a commensurate level of wisdom. Technical prowess can*not* and should *not* be considered the equivalent of wisdom. At the end of the day, technology only makes the world smaller and allows us to express ourselves and work through issues that have not changed for millennia. Basic elemental truths make us who we are: utterly human and unfortunately faulted.

All that to say, the reality is that the Founding Fathers experienced what it was like to live under the heavy hand of tyranny. They took the time to deliberate, argue and design a system of governance that recognized that the true purpose of government is to restrain, not to be the ultimate tool in the assertion of one group over another.   They built the box, and there are ample contemporary records that demonstrate that their darkest fears were that people would walk out of the safety zone they worked so hard to create.

Thus, to suggest that what they had to say about Government is not applicable in today's "modern world" is unseemly, prideful and naive.

Chapter Four:
How they work with resources

"Arbitrary power is most easily established on the ruins of liberty abused to licentiousness."
~President George Washington

Value. Commodities. Both suggest the concept of exchange something of value in order to gain something else of use or value. Money is nothing more than a measure of value and it is representative of the perceived value for whatever is sold or purchased.

Consider for a moment what churches and the Government do with money. How do they use it? How do they acquire it? How do they view it?

One might make the argument that both Government and church are made up of people, and as a result, is some of the reason for the blurring of lines and confusion between them. However, the reality is that our churches and our communities, business, religious, or otherwise, while they certainly use resources, ought to be creating more value than they take in. On the other hand, Government cannot give anything that it has not already taken away from you.

Many in our Government would like you to think that they create value with their programs; but there is not a single program running, which is not fueled by what has already been taken from you, or will be in the future. Future? Precisely, the future is being stolen by the present and supposedly is justified by the past. This is our current fiscal and monetary policy in action, currently designed and operated by the Government.

Churches and our communities should be creating value. They ought to be part of the process that lends itself to the multiplicative leveraging of resources where the whole is always greater than the individual parts...

Organisms Produce

Communities produce, whether it is church or what one traditionally considers to be a community, they should not stagnate. What do they produce? Church communities produce a sense of belonging based on a common understanding of the "meaning of life." American has meaning. Coloradoan has meaning. New Yorker ... whether it is a geography, a membership or an affiliation, the names of groups bring to mind accents, work habits, how we relate to one another, and a myriad of other things.

Nevertheless, communities produce value in terms of goods and services. People move in and out of communities for a wide range of reasons, but part of the complex formula that they apply when choosing where to live includes proximity to work. We work in order to provide for our families. We provide for our families so that we can contribute to the communities in which we live. We live in communities and associate by choice with any range of organizations based upon the things that we value: Sierra Club, Boy Scouts of America, political parties, political activism, Methodist, Buddhist, Catholic, and so on.

How does your church operate? What is the value that it produces? Can you really, and truly, say that the church you attend is multiplying its resources? How does a church multiply what is given to it? By whose measure is it multiplying, and on what grounds is that claim made? It most cases, churches are involved in redistributing that which is given to them, but in many cases does not grow, in actuality, that which they were given.

Our churches ought to be equipping people to be more complete and better wholes of themselves in order that each can better contribute the unique talents and skills they intrinsically own, skills they have purposefully developed, and the talents that they uniquely express. Thus, properly positioned, a church combines the unique aspects of their members in a new way not previously seen. The end result ought to be a community within a community that leverages its resources; people – time – money, to strengthen the greater community within which it resides.

The common problem is that many churches are broken in their ability to produce. Instead, they consume. Rather than being focused on the community in which they reside, they are inward focused. As a result, they consume the resources of their parts in order to grow the physical aspects of the church itself. Rather than being outward focused, they put restrictions on the use of resources, and rather than simply meeting the needs that are presented they question whether resources ought to be applied or not.

In this way, they are more like Government organizationally than the church as-community ought to be.

Organizations Consume

Government consumes because it cannot create value. There is no inherent ability within Government to produce a greater whole from the parts it consumes. American Federal Government has been designed as a forum for the protection of rights, and as a result, it should only consume that which contributes to the preservation and enhancement of freedom. Government is not the source of rights. It recognizes and restricts those rights. The Founders created a box that should have retained its originally designed shape.

Yet what do we see? The list is long and tawdry ... Medicaid, Medicare, TARP, ARRA, RCRA, CRA, ARA, Social Security ... you know how the list directly affects you, don't you? Not really, think of torture with paper - death by a thousand cuts. The citizens of this country are being bled dry through a thousand and one ways from taxes to fees to registration to certification... It all sounds so reasonable, does it not? But, at the end of the day, there is no real contribution to the greater good. It only removes value from the individuals of the many and varied communities around the country leaving us with diminished value and a continually diminishing sense of participation in the process.

When the Government steps into the area of the creation of value, it only drains value. The Government *IS* the proverbial black hole. It is *THE* inexorable and unstoppable force, that slows down time, alters perception of reality, and captures everything even light [life] itself.

Chapter Five:
How they build & work with teams

"Democracy is two wolves and a lamb voting on what to have for lunch. Liberty is a well-armed lamb contesting the outcome of the vote." **~Benjamin Franklin**

You may have heard the phrase, "TEAM: Together Everyone Achieves More!" Or another one, "JUICE: Join Us In Creating Excitement!" The complex interrelationships of communities within communities, that are parts of larger groups moving to the state level, the national level, and the global interaction of nations is an impossibly complex structure of communities and the relationships between them all. What everyone fails to realize is that every complex system breaks down into smaller systems that are eventually comprised of their own separate, distinct, individual pieces.

According to historians, only 2% of the total population of the original thirteen (13) colonies was actively involved in the American Revolution. In other words, the active participation of a few was able to determine the path and movement of the greater whole. Today the Lesbian-Gay-Bisexual-Transgender (LGBT) Community represents less than 3% of the entire American population, yet this powerful and vocal minority has been able to move the behavioral choice of a few from a sideline conversation to the mainstream headlines of today's news and politics.

The moral of both stories is that the groups, of which we are part, can have an incredibly powerful effect. That effect will only occur if it is properly leveraged. In order for leverage to be wielded, then we must mobilize our group to move beyond the immediate sphere of its limited perception. *Therein lies the rub.*

Are you, as a member of whatever group competing for everything with everyone? If you are, then the odds are that you will not be able to maximize the exposure of your message. Failing to properly leverage relationships and messaging to societally multiply your impact disempowers the whole. Focus the message and you will magnify its effect.

The success of the American (Colonial) Revolution enables us to consider the reality of our current religious, political and economic reality. During the time of the American Revolution, there were religious leaders, pastors and priests, who made the argument that revolution was right before God. They even called it an obligation, whereas others would focus on the demand for loyalty to God and King instead of revolt. Isn't it ironic that in multiple conflicts throughout history, both sides have proclaimed that Divine Providence has called them to their position?

Carried within the concept of team, or organized groups, one finds self-governance in action on a micro-scale. The American

Experiment, as it has been so fondly called, brings to the fore the problem of the elite who would rule, balanced by the needs of the vast majority.   Our cultural drive for independence finds its expression in so many different aspects of our lives: the small business, the family farm, the family business, the entrepreneur, the artist, the musician, the independent non-denominational church, the village, the city, the county, the parish ...

If we accept that government is inherently local, then we must come to a common understanding of what is appropriate both organizationally with government, and organically speaking when it comes to our churches. Further, we must be aware of the teams, or groups, formally organized or not, that seek to wield influence upon our governance and our churches. If we apathetically allow the motivated to dictate the course of our polity and our faith, we may find that we are unhappy with the effect they produce.

Organisms are interconnected

Individuals that collaborate together in groups and are interconnected create a multiplicative effect by leveraging strengths, and mitigating weaknesses. An organism in terms of its definition can be understood as "parts that work together to carry on the various processes of life" or "A system regarded as analogous in its structure or functions to a living body"[3]. Whether we consider the word "system" or "parts that work together," both definitions carry the understanding that there are multiple pieces that make up the whole.

Communities are inherently organic. When communities are allowed to develop appropriately, whether as a church or as a smaller geographic location (i.e. town or village), they create an interconnectedness that is the bedrock strength of this nation. Organisms grow and develop because that is their nature.

Organisms easily move resources to where they are needed. Organizations are inherently inefficient due to their lack of connectivity.

It makes sense that an organism would be interconnected as it is necessary in order for resources (a.k.a. nutrients) to get to the various parts of the body (whole). Additionally, connection is necessary for healing, in order to move restorative and healing supplies to wounded areas. What does not make sense is for a group that ought to be

---

[3] The American Heritage® Dictionary of the English Language, Fourth Edition copyright ©2000 by Houghton Mifflin Company. Updated in 2009. Published by Houghton Mifflin Company. All rights reserved.

operating as an organism to instead operate primarily as an organization.

Organizations are disconnected

Organizations are not designed for the multiplication of effort, they are designed to control and minimize the effects of individuals and groups within the group-at-large and create some level of homogeneity. Organizations are based on commonalities and a uniformity of purpose. It is the question of how homogenous we ought to be that creates such angry disagreement in our society today. To those on the left, be they liberal or truly leftist-Marxists, they have come to believe that equality means everyone is the same and should therefore be at the very same level. The only caveat to this sameness is that there are the ruling elite who determine what that sameness should be. Aspects of cultural anti-diversity can be found in such diverse societies as North Korea and Iran.

There are many who would argue that organizations are not disconnected. Nevertheless, I submit to you that there is a difference between connection due to proximity and a wholly integrated connection. Mexico, the United States, and Canada are all connected. However, they are also disconnected. Their governments are, their infrastructures are, and in fact, everything about them is disconnected in terms of how they function as entities independent of one another. They have the capacity to determine things for themselves without needing to get the "buy-in" or "permission" from anyone else.

Within organizations themselves, decisions are made in accordance with leadership. It is not typically required to get the permission or acceptance of separate departments in order for decisions to be made, or for initiatives to be implemented. The interconnectedness of departments within organizations is incidental, they are not critical to function. If necessary, departments can and often do operate as separate entities with minimal contact with others.

Effective organizations can deliver value, and they may even grow, however their growth is typically the result of their response to the efforts coordinated by leadership. Growth in an organization is not normally organic. As a matter of course, when one considers the appropriate nature of government and the appropriate nature of church, a reasonable question to consider is whether government should be organic and whether churches ought to be organizational?

In terms of their ability to create, motivate and/or develop groups or teams, Government restrains and controls. When it creates a group or a team, the purpose of the team is to study, analyze, monitor, control or otherwise restrain whatever groups or teams it has been created to address. Some might try to argue that social services create value.

Reality Check: Social services, which is one way that represents how the Government attempts to act as an organism and fails miserably in the process. Instead, it barely manages to come off as a pseudo-organism. Social services represent the Government's insertion of itself into areas of social need and social responsibility. Why? There are many reasons; the most significant reasons are as follows:

- Government has demanded that churches step aside.

- Churches have acquiesced and abdicated their responsibilities in this arena.

- Individuals no longer step forward and individualism is under attack.

- We have a cultural dichotomy where some take responsibility for themselves, and others feel that society should take care of them. This conflict is creating a cancerous malaise, a general societal unwillingness, wherein people do not get involved in meeting the needs of others. We are suffering from a collective indifference towards individuals in need.

- People have decided that societally it is more convenient to allow "someone else" to care for those who have needs. Historically, this was the domain of the church and the family however, over the last 100 years it has increasingly come to mean the Government.

Government cannot manage to work with teams with any sort of efficiency. The Government is too large to do anything efficiently. Unfortunately, this has come to be inclusive not only of spending money, but it is now true of our legislative process, of our judicial system, and of an executive branch gone awry. There are a few things that government manages to excel at and those include, spending money faster than it can be created, blowing things up, infringing the rights of others, and of course simply moving in and destroying the lives of those they deem desperate, dangerous, or simply inconvenient to achieving whatever aim is deemed the "flavor of the day."

It is certainly true that Government grows. While it grows, it does so to the denigration of its citizens. As Government grows, it must of necessity take more resources from those it governs in order to sustain itself. Revolution and the overthrow of governments occur, not simply because people are unhappy with the job that government does. Rather they are unhappy with what Government requires of them in order to do what Government does to sustain itself.

Few realize that a significant aspect of the success of the Revolutionary War was that the British Government was asking more than the American Colonies were willing to pay. The cry of "no taxation without representation" was simply emblematic of a deeper and core resentment built around the idea: "Me thinks thou dost ask too much!"

Our churches have been slowly and inexorably washed out of the "business" of caring for others as those who claim to be non-religious have seen the inefficiencies of the organizational expression of the Church in various churches themselves, individually. This is the direct result of an onslaught of secular humanism that suggests man can do just fine without God.

Additionally, as churches have been slowly and continually removed from the process of caring for the less fortunate, many of these same churches have responded in an organizational manner rather than in an organic manner.

Chapter Six:
What the impact is on their environment

*"Loyalty to a petrified opinion never broke a chain
or freed a human soul."*
~ Mark Twain

Few would argue that people impact their environment. Most in the current political environment focus on is an assumed general impact of humans on our physical environment. There is a significant movement that is attempting to justify and support claims of anthropogenic climate change. This is a very fancy way of saying that we, as humans, are changing our climate because we are so numerous and we are making so many bad decisions. This chapter is not being set to debate the merits or demerits of "global warming," "climate change" or some concept that says man is somehow harming "mother nature." If you would like to read a few thoughts concerning the environment, please review the essay regarding Christians and the environment in the last bonus chapter of this book.

This chapter really focuses on the nature of the relationship of the group to the individuals and vice versa. If we consider that individuals comprise the group as a whole, then we can understand that the group is not synonymous with its self-organizing expression as a group, a sentiment often expressed in its name. In other words, groups are not strictly defined by their name but the labels themselves may very well carry significant emotional and psychological connotations. An excellent negative example would be the variety of reactions to names like racist, Nazi, Aryan (White) Supremacist, and the KKK. The representative nature of names symbolically can typify the impact of that organization on its environment.

As individuals join or leave a group, the dynamics of that specific group adjust to the presence or absence of those individuals. This is one way to understand the concepts that drive group dynamics. The internal environment of a particular group is made of their interpersonal relationships corporately and individually. Their interactions as a whole, with other groups, comprise their external environment.

The group is not their name. How they got their name, whether inherited, acquired or otherwise ascribed, may or may not be related to their environment. Their name was created so as to identify that group. At its simplest level, their name is representative of what that group presents to those outside of the group. A specific group can be interpreted and understood separately from the context of any one individual or smaller subset of individuals from that group. However, it is important to understand how the group as a whole reacts to, interacts with, or works in conjunction with the parts (or individuals) that comprise the whole.

Understanding how a group works within its context means that one can begin to understand the impact they have. While not absolutely definitive, names allow us to categorize, systematize and organize our environment. The vast multitude of different groups creates the environment within which we all operate. In short, seeing the various pieces helps us to begin to grasp the diversity of the system that is our community and to a lesser extent our society as a whole. This is the environment within which our churches and Government operate.

Organisms are synergistic and/or symbiotic

It is important to recognize that there is an aspect that is not in any way related to a New Age Philosophy, or a Worship of Mother Earth perspective, in which one can appreciate and understand both synergy and symbiotic in a relational context. One of the challenges in a modern day world is that the context and definition of words in their cultural application are not always truly representative of the baseline, and sometimes perhaps deeper, meanings of those words.

When we make the statement that organisms are synergistic, what does that really mean? The American Heritage Dictionary defines synergy as "The interaction of two or more agents or forces so that their combined effect is greater than the sum of their individual effects"[4]. It is within this basic definition that we understand what an organic approach to understanding what healthy group dynamics ought to look like. Broadening the concept somewhat to our current setting, a synergistic group is one where the group benefits from the individual and the individual benefits from association with the group.

When a group chooses to take from the individual whatever the individual is willing to offer, or perhaps forces the individual to surrender something in order to be a part of the group, then synergy ceases. It ceases because, while the group benefits as a whole in this scenario, the individual does not benefit. Another way to show this lack of benefit, is when members assert that association with the

---

[4] The American Heritage® Dictionary of the English Language, Fourth Edition copyright ©2000 by Houghton Mifflin Company. Updated in 2009. Published by Houghton Mifflin Company.

group is beneficial to the individual, thus assuming the individual will feel an obligation to sacrifice for them and the group as a whole.

Some might argue that the individual cannot become part of a group without sacrificing or giving something up in return for that association. This moves the question from one of mutual benefit to one of mutually beneficial sacrifice. While it is reasonable to suggest that participating in a group of some kind carries a cost, it is unfortunate that many are either unwilling or unable to count that cost. Frequently decisions are made by us, for us, or even forced upon us in spite of our choices to the contrary.

Cost can be measured in so many different ways. We measure cost in terms of time spent, in terms of money (a.k.a. financial resources), in terms of shared expertise, or perhaps in terms of our willingness to surrender our rights. The question is whether or not we have knowingly agreed to pay the cost. Too often groups ask members to pay a price without really quantifying or explaining what that cost represents both to them and to the group. Instead, they make the assumption that the members should intuitively understand their perception of what they believe is inherently best for all. The reality is that few articulate the cost, and few still understand the full implications of the impacts of those costs.

When we make the statement that organisms are symbiotic, what does that really mean? The American Heritage Dictionary defines symbiotic as being "A relationship of mutual benefit or dependence" and more specifically as an adjective that is "used of organisms (especially of different species) living together but not necessarily in a relation beneficial to each"[5]. Clearly the term symbiotic is not precisely interchangeable with synergistic, and it is most importantly in the emphasis of the word that we find a greater understanding that meets the purpose.

Organisms, when they are comprised of self-organizing and self-governing groups of people, are symbiotic in the way that a body is comprised of parts that cannot function independently of one another. Each organ, or part, of the body has a specific designed function that makes up its role in the body. The hand can pump, but it cannot pump blood within the body. The lungs breathe for the body, but

---

[5] The American Heritage® Dictionary of the English Language, Fourth Edition copyright ©2000 by Houghton Mifflin Company. Updated in 2009. Published by Houghton Mifflin Company.

they cannot move oxygen throughout the body so that the rest of the body "breathes." You can walk on your hands if you are physically fit, but your hands were not made for walking.

When part of the body is asked to fill a role that it was not designed for the body endures stress. Sometimes, due to injury, loss or defect a body must operate without a designed part simply in order to function. Depending on the body, that may or may not be sustainable in the long term. For an amazing story about what is possible visit YouTube: http://www.youtube.com/watch?v=H8ZuKF3dxCY. This is a brief seven-minute video that provides a brief overview of the story of Nick Vujicic from Australia. He was born to Christian parents with no arms, no legs, and his only limb is part of one foot. Yet, despite being unbelievably physically challenged, he tells how he moved from being ready to commit suicide to pursuing all that he can squeeze out of life.

This amazing inspirational story shows us what is possible, but it does not address that there are things without which the body simply cannot survive. Many groups that should be organically thriving bodies, are instead much more like Nick Vujicic, doing amazing things with important pieces missing.

Organizations are parasitic

Organizations by their very nature are parasitic. Government is not capable of being anything other than a parasite. The key to responsible government is ensuring that it stays small. When it stays small, the "body" of the population survives. When it becomes too large, the life of the body is threatened. A simple definition of parasite is "One who habitually takes advantage of the generosity of others without making any useful return"[6].

Many will throw their hands and arms up in disgust at the suggestion that organizations are parasitic. Why? Because, they argue, that organizations whether they are religious, non-profit or governmental provide benefits to their constituents, participants or customers whoever they be. However, when one considers the amount of interaction that an individual may have had with their government 100 years ago or even 150 years ago, the realization sets

---

[6] The American Heritage® Dictionary of the English Language, Fourth Edition copyright ©2000 by Houghton Mifflin Company. Updated in 2009. Published by Houghton Mifflin Company.

in that government is far more intrusive in our lives today than it was before.

In the American experiment, the primary benefit to self-governance was supposed to be the guarantee of protection afforded to the citizenry through the Bill of Rights, also known as (a.k.a.) the first ten amendments. In concert with the Constitution, the Bill of Rights provides a series of negative propositions which government shall not transgress, and it enumerates the powers afforded to the various sections of the government: executive, legislative and judicial. Most, if not all, of the states have something similar constructed at the state level. However, since the establishment of these documents as the supreme understanding of our protections for the expression of our freedoms through self-governance, the law of entropy has settled into the political process.

Entropy has set, in the sense that, politics has continued to devolve from the protection of our freedoms, to the assertion of beliefs. Those beliefs have included the demasculinization of our inner cities through welfare programs, the disemboweling of charities and churches by mandating government handouts, and the slow onset of lifestyle laws some of which lend themselves towards the infringements of our Constitutionally guaranteed rights, especially as they relate to the 1st and 2nd Amendments.

While Government may genuinely, at some level, follow through on many of its responsibilities. It is the abject failure to meet many more, coupled with an unbridled penchant for taxation and spending that lends itself to the appellation of Parasite rather than being either synergistic or symbiotic. At the same time, Government was never designed to be anything more than what it is - parasitic. However, a small parasite does not threaten the body and produces little to minor harm. The same cannot be said of Government today.

In the same vein, many churches fall into the trap of being organizational and thus parasitic instead of aligning themselves as organisms. The beauty of a church body is that when it is properly aligned spiritually it contributes to the overall quality of life both within and without its immediate community. Too many churches, however, focus on taking from the body what they need in order to perpetuate their programs and facilities and as a result maintain a myopic inward focus. This is demonstrated by statements from pastors that say things like "It's your job to bring people in, and my job to tell them the truth about God" (*overheard from the pulpit one*

Sunday morning). Other ways this may be seen is the emphasis on program to the distraction from individuals within the church body.

A church ought to be synergistically symbiotic in both its conception and expression. Government is necessarily parasitic, but it should not be dangerously overwhelming to its constituency.

Chapter Seven:
Ability to be transparent

"Thoughts lead on to purposes;
purposes go forth in action;
actions form habits;
habits decide character;
and character fixes our destiny."
~Tryon Edwards

The differences between darkness and light are voluminous. People have spoken about the conflict between good and evil, dark versus light, ignorance versus knowledge, hidden versus revealed and so on for centuries. What should be talked about, but is not necessarily discussed is the tendency for organizations to be closed. Their tendency to keep, even their own members, "in the dark" so to speak concerning what is happening within their group is more common than most would like to admit.

Organizations, or groups, that have a tendency to make decisions and then act providing information to the rank and file as an apparent post script will see those moves result in a variety of deleterious impacts. People experience the range of emotion from indifference, to surprise and even anger depending upon their level of awareness of the issues within their group. The level of intensity they express their emotions with will typically depend upon how transparent the group has been with them.

The level of intensity in their reactions will also directly correlate to their belief in their ability to impact the decision and its eventual outcome. The more helpless they feel, and the more they feel that their situation has been taken advantage of, the stronger their negative reactions are likely to be. Thus, the willingness and ability of an organization to manage to be transparent, the less resistance they will likely face.

Organisms, on the other hand, do not function well without light. In fact, depending on the organism, with some biological exceptions, the vast majority of the species on earth require light for simple survival. While it is true that there are, species found in caves and in the deepest depths of the ocean where light cannot penetrate, those species are the exception to the rule. Allow some creative license and roll with the illustration.

There has been a great deal of discussion in the last few years regarding the need for transparency in governance. Why? The thought line is that if back room dealings are opened to the "light" of public notice and opinions then perhaps those deals will be more advantageous to the public that they are supposed to serve. However, by and large, most deals are cut in the dark rooms which surround the various halls of power and politics because it would seem that most of the political elite do not believe that the average person has a "need-to-know" and in some cases would argue that the "average person" would not understand the need for compromise.

A failure to provide transparency means that members of the group are functioning without understanding the entire context. A failure to understand context is very similar to a body that suffers from paralysis. The ability of the body to communicate with itself enables it to function properly. Paralysis is the result of a failure to communicate. Not because the group cannot take action, but because it is not acting based on all of the information in the environment. For example, if someone with paralysis was to have their feet too close to a fire, they could get burned and not even know it!

This kind of paralysis where communication within the body or the organization is blocked is a significant contributing factor leading to a failure of both churches and Government today. In the church, the failure to be able to foster and maintain open lines of communication means that when others in the church body are hurting, or damaged, the rest of the body fails to respond because the natural mechanism to communicate that pain is missing, damaged, or blocked.

Government, more generically, lacks the openness that would reduce the abusive extravagance that our legislative process currently endures. It is further obscured and harmed by the excesses of executive "orders" and judicial "review." A failure to shine the "light" of public inquiry into our governance has been the direct result of a deadly combination of trust and apathy of the governed on the one hand, and the secretive abuse on the part of those who govern.

Organisms are open

Organisms exist and they benefit their various parts by their existence. At some level, most organisms do have anything to hide, especially from itself. Most are willing to accept that there is a manner in which an organism can be analyzed and understood as being a collection of systems, or parts. However, everyone would also agree that "whole-istically" the sum of the parts is greater than the parts in and of themselves.

Continuing with the concept and importance of keeping the internal lines of communication open, one can understand that it is simply deadly to not maintain those ready and open lines of communication. A failure to be fully functioning means that the organism has to alter how it functions in order to accommodate the lack of clarity. That lack of clarity means that the organism will not be able to reach its full potential.

From a practical standpoint, when one considers the organic nature of church organisms, it is important to understand that communication includes a willingness to allow for discussion and debate. The Jewish community is one of the most adept communities at allowing for discussion and debate, without necessarily throwing the question of the existence of God and our relationship to him to the vagaries of the winds of opinion.

If churches are to maintain their open lines of communication, part of that process needs to be reflected in the centuries of tradition that allow each generation to explore and coming to understand what it means to be spiritual. A lack of willingness to entertain the discussion means that there will be those who are simply ostracized for their desire for discussion and debate. Thus, the pedantic and overbearing presentation of a religious view can come across as being discursive regarding the various parts of the body, including those prone to discuss and question.

Allowing a forum for discussion and debate is not the same thing as throwing distinctive and core principles to the wind. Typically debate centers more around practice, than around the key tenets of the body. In the case of Christians, the key tenets would include the sanctity of Scripture, the existence of the Trinity, the sacrifice of Christ, and necessity of unity in love.

While this is not specifically designed to be an apologetic work for Christianity, it should be noted that many denominations, as well as other forms of religion, have a tendency to become institutionalized and dictatorial, rather than communal. The result is that there is a lack of transparent discussion regarding the "who" and the "why" of the "how." The continual erosion of an emphasis on ensuring the value of the individual parts that comprise the whole results in a general degradation of both faith and practice.

Rejecting discussion and debate creates a kind of paralysis in terms of the body's ability to communicate with itself, to say nothing of the outside world. The sickness of institutional inertia creates a body that is weak and unable to meet the challenges it faces. The unfortunate result being that its extremities become sick, infected, or may even die as a result of the failure to communicate ope

Organizations are protective (a.k.a. closed)

Organisms are protective and so are organizations. But, the way in which they protect and the things which they protect are vastly different. Organisms exist to benefit the parts of the whole. The organization exists to benefit itself. Typically, an organization presents its drive to benefit itself as being the drive to benefit all of the parts. Unfortunately, the resulting benefit is really derived to just a few. Frequently, the few in an organization that benefit are those in power, or leadership. The "head" of the organization, rather than the body as a whole, is frequently what benefits most. When it comes to politics however, the benefit has been passed down to those who are seemingly bereft of opportunity, but only to the extent that they will support the ruling elite.

Organizations are dismissive of the contribution of the average individual member. The regular and consistent application of effort which produces a measurable result does not equate to the respect that service is due. Rather in organizations, whether governmental or religious, it is the rank and file that are seen as simply rank, and therefore less valuable. While most in both of these kinds of organizations would say that they exist to serve those folks, the reality is they are unwilling to share the details with those folks. It is their unwillingness to be transparent and open that demonstrates their lack of respect.

Rules & Religion: *Wrecking America*

Most people are familiar with when Congresswoman Pelosi irresponsibly stated "But we have to pass the bill so you can find out what is in it" regarding the Patient Protection and Affordable Care Act (PPACA), commonly referred to as "Obamacare" (http://www.youtube.com/watch?v=KoE1R-xH5To). As the details of what is in the bill have been coming to light, it is apparent that a number of side deals and back room deals were made in order to get this bill passed into law. If you want to know more, just Google it and you will find all sorts of data on just this one bill. This demonstrates the complete lack of respect that many politicians have for their constituents.

The closed organization ... a.k.a. back-room deals ... a.k.a. those of influence who wield more interest and concern than those who are concerned, but seem to lack financial resources ... all of these characteristics are emblematic of the closed organization. They are un-courteous and dismissive in their concern for the members. If they valued the rank and file, then they would trust them with the details and make the processes open for scrutiny and debate. The continuing and habitual failure underlines the elitist mentality, rather than the inclusion of all in the process of debate.

For some reason, the elite, whether spiritual or political, seem to believe that stifling debate is somehow healthy. While it is true that a governmental organization cannot really function effectively as an organism, there is certainly no truth to the unspoken assertion that eliminating discussion somehow equals the protection of those that they are supposed to serve.

Most understand that change and policy and function of large groups occurs much more efficiently and effectively when time and care is placed upon the efforts to create understanding, provide for input and debate, resulting in a plan that takes into account the appropriate perspectives of those concerned.

However, both our churches and our Government have consistently demonstrated they are absolutely unconcerned with the buy-in of even those in opposition to their point of view. The fact that there is such discord indicates that there has been a serious breach of communication with the bulk of the population. Government has been non-productively closed in its processes, which is creating a rising level of frustration. As politicians run pell-mell in directions directly opposite to that which the majority of Americans deem sane and reasonable, there is also a commensurate "closure" of communication as the process has been removed from the public eye. That any politician would call themselves a public servant, and then demand passage of a piece of legislation "so that we can see what is in it" is foolish, irresponsible and derelict in their duty to the people.

While Government cannot operate as an organism, its role as a limiting force in society must therefore be open to scrutiny. Not because of any pseudo-organic initiative, but because the people which they are to be serving have every right to understand exactly what is happening so that they may be educated on the prospective impact of proposed legislation and/or initiatives.

Chapter Eight:
Ability to empower those who struggle

"Problems call forth our courage and our wisdom, indeed they create our courage and wisdom. It is only because of problems that we grow. It is for this reason that wise people learn not to dread but actually welcome problems."
~M. Scott Peck

"The credit belongs to the man who is actually in the arena, whose face is marred by dust and sweat and blood, who strives valiantly, who errs and comes short again and again, who knows the great enthusiasms, the great devotions, and spends himself in a worthy cause, who at best knows achievement and who at the worst if he fails at least fails while daring greatly so that his place shall never be with those cold and timid souls who know neither victory nor defeat."
~Theodore Roosevelt

"Children are apt to live up to what you believe of them."
~Lady Bird Johnson

We need to remember that there is a quantitative and a qualitative difference between empowering and enabling. Neither churches nor the government grasp the critical distinction between these words. While both of those words may be used similarly, one centers on "able" and the other centers on "power." Turning these concepts on their side, one ought to consider who has the "power" when the word is used, and how is that power expressed? Power really communicates impact, and the ability to determine direction. Whereas "able" is similar to "ability," both of which speak to the potential, but not the actualization, or implementation, or execution of that "able"-ness.

The words are somewhat deceiving in and of themselves. On the one hand, one would think that "empowering" people might have a negative connotation and that "enabling" people would be positive. Certainly, it would seem that both words carry such similar connotations, why bother drawing a difference? Let us consider the context in which these words are often used.

The word "enable" is frequently used in the context of furthering someone in his or her pursuit of a less than positive For example, many feel that welfare enables people in their dependency on government rather than empowering them to make a difference in their own lives. Empower is a word that carries the pack of a fully wound punch. It is not just ability, it is the fully energized thrust to carry through on something that must be done.

Churches today can be accused of enabling people in their victimology such that, the person who commits a wrong is either cast as incapable of making right decisions, or is simply cast out and ostracized from the general context of that community. It happens frequently enough in Christian circles that Christians are often accused of "shooting their wounded." In other words, instead of extending grace and empowering that victim to work through either their bad decisions or the powerfully negative actions of someone else, they walk down "the other side of the street" and avoid them as though they had the plague.

Government is even worse. Government allows the enabling of the poor performance of the poor in so many different ways that the poor seem doomed to break the chains of poverty. Make no mistake the Government wounds the very identity of the people it proposes to help such that the person is marred. It damages confidence and independence so badly that few it seems are able to escape the trap of

Government services.   Rather than embracing the humanity of empowerment, they indiscriminately scatter the seeds of enablement in such programs as public service unions (i.e. teacher unions), welfare and other forms of so-called public assistance.

The problem is that for the vast majority of Americans struggling below the poverty line, they have come to believe that they cannot provide enough value to anyone to ever be worth more than the pittance they are parceled out from the vast social services empire. Our social services have created such a disservice, that the average person dependent upon these services is dis-incentivized to lift themselves from the miry clay of want and need.

This is a general wound against the psyche of the average person. Nevertheless, it is also a specific dagger pointed at the heart of every man and woman whose family must rely upon the government more than his or her own ability to provide.   This reliance is beyond the bounds of the emergency service provided through unemployment benefits, or short-term assistance. This reliance is a devastating malaise created by a long-term dependence upon charity of the state.

For some reason, it would appear that many churches and the Government seem to expect self-healing, but they have been completely inept at defining a program or providing a service that moves people from dependence to independence. The failure to teach one generation how to be independent is to create a larger generation that understands only dependence. The legacy of dependence has become entitlement. As we move into now the fourth plus generation since the overwhelming surge of "social services," the lower middle class is now on the verge of slipping below the poverty level and the upper class is becoming more distinct, and distinctly smaller.

Some would argue that this is a reason to push for greater disbursement of "economic parity" through the hyper-taxation of the rich in order to supplement the entitlements to the poor. The democratic mortar that is slowly eroding from our Republican foundation has been breached in such a way that our Republican form of government is at risk. With the runaway pandering to a generation brainwashed to believe that it is entitled to receive, more than it is obligated to give or create, means that there are fewer and fewer in succeeding generations willing to stand up and chase the American Dream.

The American Dream is ably defined and framed by many different races and creeds. This dream boils down to one essential and peculiar truth; rewarding the hard work of the dedicated and sacrificial elite. Unfortunately, our tax-and-welfare system is creating a crab pot of national proportions. How so?

Consider, do you know why there is no need to put a lid on a pot full of crabs? It is quite simple really. As soon as one tries to climb out, the others pull the climber back down in order to have their own go at it. Thus, instead of working together to create a way out, they end up destroying each other in the process. This is the reality of our tax-and-welfare spending system.

Organisms release healing

If it is not uncommon for churches to be seen as shooting their wounded, the irony is that it flies in the face of the promise of healing. People typically flock to houses of worship, of whatever stripe, in order to find answers to the deeper questions in life and hope for healing wounds that trail beneath the deepest surfaces of their lives. While many organisms understand how to provide healing to the wounded parts of itself the average church seems incapable of releasing the necessary resources in the appropriate and timely fashion. What is the result? Many are dashed upon the rocks of despair within view of the lighthouse of hope. The only problem - someone forgot to turn on the light.

Part of empowerment is being able to move past what has injured or harmed one in the past. Organisms physically are capable of working so they pull out all the stops out moving that body from injured to as fully functional as possible, as quickly as possible. In fact, many times, when the body falls asleep, it is better able to repair itself.

While churches ought to be a place where healing occurs, the reality is that most churches do not create or provide a safe environment for healing to occur. Whether one is the victimized, or the victimizer, the vast majority of those who attend church do not understand how to begin to relate to either side of that equation. There is a tendency to see the need for a paid professional to attend to the situation because they are somehow better prepared to offer a solution that deals with the problem, whether pain or tragedy or some other thing.

Healing is just the beginning of empowerment. Truly, if one desires to be empowered, they must also move past the detritus of enablement. Enablement is crippling because it essentially is very similar to what happens when one immobilizes a broken limb with a cast. The muscles atrophy because they are not used. They are not used because there is an external force that prevents them from exerting themselves.

In the case of a broken bone, this provides a safe environment to promote healing of the bones. In the case of a wounded heart, or broken person, it helps to have a strong and safe environment within which to heal. The problem in most churches, as well as with Government, is that once the time for healing has come and gone, the "cast" is never removed. As a result, the emotional, financial, or spiritual "bones" and "muscles" of that person atrophy to the point where they are utterly dependent on that "cast."

Many church organizations, and this is not limited to Christian churches, have been "hard cast" to tell people what to do, where to go, what to say, and how to live. They are incapable of helping people beyond the point of initial recovery. People heal, and then they sit, they soak, and then they sour. Then the trappings that come with that inactivity, if you have ever broken a limb then you may remember that almost vinegar-like smell that comes from being unable to wash around the cast properly. The same thing happens with attitudes and a willingness to get beyond the narrow confines of one's "immediate world." As a result, their spiritual muscles and their emotional muscles, and sometimes their verbal-inter-relational muscles all atrophy.

What is the end result? Instead of providing a healing power that releases those who were in pain to then be able to go and provide the same release for others, the "hard cast" community becomes a hindrance to the expression of the heart. The members of these groups expect someone else, the pastor, the youth pastor, the visitation pastor, the church secretary ... you name the position... they expect someone else to take up the need and seek to meet it. Perhaps the organizational expression of the Church in churches is little more than a "hard cast" which people become so dependent on that they fail to experience the empowering release of a truly connected and spirit filled person.

Then the next stage of atrophy sets in. If one cannot be relied upon to seek to meet the needs of his fellow man, but instead prefers to leave it to the paid professionals. Then, it takes no stretch of the imagination to see the benefit of having government step in to handle things. After all, what could be better than a larger, better-funded organization to step in and make sure that no one falls through the cracks!?

Organizations cover pain (and sometimes destroy those in pain)

Here is the problem with that concept. Now that the various psychological and emotional "muscles" of people have atrophied to the point where they are incapable of being of service to their fellow man, it now requires that the emotions of the individual simply be numbed. Moving and exercising them even a little bit can cause a great deal of pain. So it is when those who are used to being ignored and otherwise having nothing expected of them, suddenly find themselves faced with the need to feel and do.

It is painful and it is inconvenient. Therefore, there are a number of means that one might use as a distraction for numbing that pain. Any good physical therapist will tell you that in order to overcome apathy one must exercise and engage the pain. A failure to engage the pain means that healing and strengthening cannot occur. The point of strengthening oneself is so that one can become fully functional, and thus no longer dependent on the assistance of others.

What Government provides is a massive, yet wholly inefficient, general anesthesia called "social services." This anesthesia numbs individuals of society at all levels. It numbs individuals on the bottom of society as they find themselves unable to lift their heads from the trough of public assistance. It numbs the middle class as they are too busy trying to survive that they pay little attention to how, when, where or why their tax dollars are spent. It numbs the upper class with an excuse to "not get involved" with the "petty and pedestrian" concerns of the lower classes. "Why pay attention," they unconsciously consider, "when I am already paying so much. Let the government and the churches care for the less fortunate. After all – isn't that what we pay them for?"

However, it is important to note that this thought process began in churches where leadership made a conscious decision to function in a disengaged manner. They enfeebled their membership by not understanding how to engage them in the process of connecting with "the body-at-large." The failure of a church organization to engage its members stems from a morose collection of leaders who desire control, a membership that is flaccidly unengaged, and a group that, as a whole, has lost the language of real community.

The larger it is, especially if it is a church organization that actively serves more than 400 people each Sunday, is more likely to struggle with community engagement. Think about your church community. Do the people in your congregation make it a habit to say hello and greet as many people as they can, especially those unfamiliar faces? Or is it like most "mega" church communities where so many people run in and out the door that is very unusual to see the same people Sunday to Sunday.

Experts tell us that the average person has a circle of friends, acquaintances and family that ranges from 180 to 300 people. The sheer size of a mega church overwhelms an average person's ability to connect meaningfully with so many. As a result, the "worship" service ends up being a corporate meeting that is highly programmatic right down to the "turn and shake the person's hand standing next to you." Most people cannot recall the name of the person they shook hands with because they never even asked for it.

Now, moving forward from the failure of our churches to create real community, we now find Government attempting to fill the void. They seek to fill the void, partly at behest of liberals and extreme leftists, but also partly due to the silence of the churches. Instead of simply being "cast" in the hard and inflexible mold of a top-down focused spiritual group, the people are being numbed into ineffectiveness through all sorts of means. If an individual church group can in some ways be typified as being a "cast," then the Government when it ventures out into unconstitutional areas such as social services is acting in many ways like an intensive care unit (ICU).

In this case, the care is so intense and so invasive, that the longer one is subjected to this level of intense "care" the less able that individual is to break the mold of that care and become a fully functioning and independent member of society. The Government Elite would suggest that this level of intense care is because it is so needed. Nevertheless, the reality is that it fits a command and control concept that seeks to derail and deride any expression of faith other than secular humanism as bankrupt, inefficient and meaningless. Continually being forced to cope with this level of intense intrusion into one's life leaves one's ability to be self-responsible continually eroding towards incompetence and thus dependency.

Some might argue that Pain prohibits healing. Moreover, as we can consider it, it is true that pain does indeed at times make it difficult to heal. For example, it is nearly impossible to heal properly from broken ribs without pain reliever. Why? Because drawing your very breath is horribly painful. Shallower breaths mean inefficient oxygenation of the body, and all sorts of other problems may set in. However, the jump in logic from "Pain prevents healing" in some circumstances to being "Pain cannot be tolerated at all" is irresponsible and unsustainable. It is irresponsible because it opens the "body" of the community to deeper more intransigent pain that eventually explodes through the painkiller, regardless how many doses the victim takes. Eventually the cause of the pain or the painkillers themselves opens the victim to more sickness and even death.

Our Government was never designed to be the panacea for all that ails one from the financial to the social. Rather, the role of Government was to provide a safe haven where the individual might flex his or her own muscles and assert their relative independence within the confines of respecting the rights of others. The onset of spiritual atrophy, sometimes termed apathy, brought about at least in part by a dictatorial de-sensitizing top-down approach to spirituality created an opportune environment for the development of Government as the ICU. Government as an ICU disables, disempowers, and enfeebles the efforts of the individual in order to maintain life support for others that are "weaker" and "disadvantaged."

Consider the aftermath of a heart attack. If the patient survives, it is very common for the patient to be up and walking within 24 hours of the attack. Why? The heart is a muscle and it needs exercise. When I was in college, I was injured in an intramural basketball game. With just four seconds left on the clock, I went for a rebound missed, and another player stepped on the inside of my left foot. As my ankle rolled, briefly blacking out from the severe pain, I later learned that I had severed all three lateral ligaments in my left ankle.

Powerful pain relievers, followed by surgery a week later, and then ensconced in cast for nine weeks I was not able to really exercise my left leg for a total of nine weeks. During those nine weeks, I did everything I could to avoid feeling pain. Let's face it – pain really sucks. Following the removal of the cast, my left calf muscle had atrophied to half its former size. The cast did its job in keeping my left ankle stable so that it could heal. But, eventually the ankle had healed enough so that I could begin to use it again. Government programs are just like that cast. The problem is that LBG proponents think that the plans and programs they have conceived need to be permanent.

What most fail to realize is that the goal of some in our Government today is to destroy that which competes with their desire to implement ICU-like control of society. Destruction is sometimes the result of organizations that feel pain because they destroy what they believe is the source of that pain. However, committing to radical amputation when a simple antibiotic would have solved the problem is excessive at a minimum and deadly at a maximum. Yet, that is precisely what those in power today are doing.

Whether it is the overly controlling spiritual leader, or the overzealous political leader, both are operating under the false assumption that people are incapable of caring for themselves, of being able to produce enough value. They do not believe that individuals, if left alone in healthy community, are capable and willing of caring for their fellow man.

The source of our pain as a society is not necessarily causal in some linear fashion rather it is emblematic of the disempowerment of our Government. It is also emblematic of the enfeebling caused by our churches. Each part contributes to the whole of a society that wants to step out of the ICU. Yet our ICU-bedridden society is choking on the drugs and painkillers that include the pseudo-community of many of today's churches. We are fighting against the bed restraints of programs such as Welfare, poor Public Education, TARP, ARRA, and so many other forms of Public Programs that are simply gutting the value and strength of Lady Liberty.

Freedom of Religion and Freedom of Enterprise go hand in hand with the ability of an engaged community to meet the needs of its local "body." Organizational churches stand in opposition to this, and in practicality, Government seeks to fill this role. If the Statue of Liberty is truly emblematic of the United State and her freedoms, then Freedom of Enterprise is the blood that flows through her veins, and Freedom of Religion is the air that she breathes.

The citizens of every community represent pieces of the Body-Politic that is the United States, and churches are pieces of the Body that is the Universal Church, a.k.a. the Body of Christ. Organizationally churches need to stop interfering with the natural flow of the body and instead allow it to naturally grow and develop. The leaders of our churches need to facilitate the community of the Body of Christ, and not dictate what the body of community should look like. Instead, they choose a select few to determine who should receive what in response to a selectively limited expression of need.

Our spiritual communities should be wholly connected and in real and transparent communication that allows the hearts of individuals in the community to meet the needs of other members in the community. There is no resource problem today. The problem we face is a heart problem. We need to collect our hearts back from the leadership that we surrendered it to and begin to listen to our hearts in communion with God. If God is not the author of confusion, and if we believe that we can work out what is good and right, then we do not need someone else to tell us what that looks like. Instead of allowing someone to tell us what to give, we should respond to expressed need after meditating on it before God.

Our Government needs to get out of the ICU and become more like a family doctor. Check the diagnosis, offer a solution and then get out of the way so that the body can heal itself. The family doctor of yesteryear had a relationship with their patients, and understood the context of family history. Generally speaking, because of their familiarity with the patients and their families, they were better armed and more able to offer the best solution at the right time.

However, true doctors understand that they are not the cause of healing. Rather they see the need to remove obstacles to healing and prepare the patient so that the patient's own body can do what it must in order to fully recover. Government needs to realize and remember that it was never designed to be the cure. It was only designed to be the doctor. It's time for the doctor(s) to get out of the patient's way.

Government cannot create community. It cannot legislate community into existence. It cannot prevent all wrongs and it cannot eliminate evil. Government exists to restrain evil, thus to be a force of moderation in the community so that the pursuit of one's natural rights is not prevented by someone else's usurpation of the natural order of things.

Churches are capable of creating and growing community, but they cannot do it from the confines of their top-down leader-centric organizations. Whether it is the quasi-cult of community that rises up around a personality, or if it is simply expressed as one of the myriad forms of church governance. The problem most churches have is that their governance of resources, too often extends to a governance of theology.

As the governance of the practice of faith becomes the vitriolic source of debate, church becomes "community lost" and it finds itself choking for breath on the ICU-bed of restrictive government. They build monstrosities of massive "public service" projects euphemistically referred to as a "campus" and they see their impact on their larger communities dissipate, as their focus becomes facility and program over and above individual people, families and their needs.

In summary, Government soothes and numbs the pain through "social services" and "public works" projects and the like. However, churches are just as guilty by excising the heart of their community members in favor of programs and facilities.

Chapter Nine:
Willingness to allow for self-direction

*"Even a mistake may turn out to be the one thing necessary
to a worthwhile achievement."*
~Henry Ford

*"I'm a firm believer that in the theory that people only do their best
at things they truly enjoy. It is difficult to excel
at something you don't enjoy."*
~Jack Nicklaus

Dictatorial versus self-direction, is it possibly that simple? When one is self-directed, then one has the ability to directly impact the course and influence of one's life. Whereas a dictator dictates, and thus directs others meaning that his, or her, life determines the course of the lives of others through the enforcement of one's influence on as many aspects as possible. Right now, you and I have a choice. We have the ability to choose a government and a society that allows us the freedom of self-governance and self-defined purpose.

However, should we continue to allow our institutions, both religious and governmental, to have the ability to dictate what our lives should look like? If we do, then we will continue to see the loss of personal freedoms. It is tragic to realize that some people today, with only a basic understanding of the last 2000 years of history seem to think that different expressions of faith through the ages has been a reason for a lack of freedom, and at times, periods of intellectual darkness. If that carries some truth, and it does, then why would that be sad? It is tragic because too many of us think that this is no longer true.

Nothing could be further from the truth. Faith is such an integral part of life that our form of governance is directly tied to our dominant faith reasoning. In the early centuries after Jesus Christ, consider that the Caesars presented themselves as gods, and thus as the only ones capable of rule. In the middle ages, the divine right of kings, a Christianized version of the same concept prevailed. Now, as the 21st Century gathers momentum, there is a significant battle occurring in the United States between the dominant religious philosophy called Secular Humanism and those of Faith. Any Secular Humanist that tries to deny that their philosophy of life is not religious is lying to themselves and anyone they say it to. It takes just as much faith to believe that God does not exist, as it does to say that He does.

The irony is that Secular Humanism stands upon a pillar of so-called tolerance, but it is not willing to be tolerant of a worldview that includes the concepts of sin and an Almighty God. A decidedly Judeo-Christian bias was at the heart of the American Revolution and it found its ultimate expression in the Bill of Rights. The Ten Commandments are a series of 10 "thou shalt nots." It is God's original guide for how we as humans relate to Him and to each other.

The Bill of Rights is a series of "thou shalt nots" for how Government relates to its citizens. Despite this history, our society today enjoys an outright assault on all things of faith and at the same time, our freedoms are continually being eroded.

The vast underlying basis of liberty, law and basic right and wrong find their basis in the Ten Commandments and a Judeo-Christian ethic. While the Secular Humanist may argue that the norms and mores of society are based on a variable scale of morality and ethics, in practicality no law written works that way. The basis of law considers that there is an absolute standard. If there were not, then anarchy would prevail. Even Sharia Law and the Qur'an find some basis in a syncretistic plagiarism of Judaism, Christianity and Zoroastrianism.

Organisms reveal and release purpose

The pursuit of happiness cannot happen in an environment where self-discovery, exploration and entrepreneurialism are discouraged, restricted or stepped upon. The power of a self-aware person pursuing their giftedness cannot find their genesis in a setting where self-determination and self-responsibility are ignored or even prevented.

Rules & Religion: *Wrecking America*

The local church community in a traditional Jewish setting finds itself continually reinventing itself as technology, government and life progress there is an ability for faith and practice to flex while still maintaining an understanding of who G-d is in the midst of it all. However, in the community of the Church there is a desperate lack of empowerment. Instead, there is a marked tendency to react negatively to the advance of change in technology, forms of worship including styles of music, and even in how we individually choose to talk to God or about him.

The organic approach to community recognizes that there is unique, intrinsic and special value in each life, regardless of intellectual, financial, emotional or athletic ability. The organic approach to community is inherently empowering and encouraging. The organic community understands how to promote self-discovery, while encouraging an exploration of who God is.

Real community understands that in order to have impact, there must be recognition of the importance of actively engaging with community members. As members interact, they are not necessarily overtly directive in their approach, nor are they necessarily directed. While it is true that there may be times where top-down direction may exist, it recognizes that this will not always be the case. Rather, this community will be bubbling up from the bottom as well. It is not just trickle down, it is bi-directional trickling – up and down.

As the organization cross utilizes resources and seeks to instill the "fertilization" of ideas, there is significant release of potential for innovation. Invention rises out of innovation and is created by releasing individuals to pursue and explore on their own without being driven toward a predetermined goal or conclusion. This is the empowerment of release to follow one's own direction.

Organizations dictate utility and determine direction

Organizations are by nature typically hierarchical. In other words, there is a top down approach to everything. The top sets the direction. The top decides what is important. The top determines how someone, or something, is useful to those who are giving the direction. The top determines how they will do what needs to be done. In short, the where, when, why, and how of an organization is dictated by those "in-charge."

Certainly one can argue that there are times of supra-ordinary circumstances where a dictatorial approach may be beneficial. However, in these types of organizations the top-down mentality has a tendency to produce two critical weaknesses 1) a silo mentality and 2) a corresponding lack of cross-functionalism. Is that good or bad? After all, there is no such thing as a "perfect" system, right?

A "silo" mentality is on the one hand completely focused, but on the other hand completely lacking in context. For example, developing a system that rapidly can sell homes by leveraging multiple forms of technology may lack the context of a current down market. A down real estate market may be marked with an erosion of value and a continually lengthening average listing before the successful and consequent sale of a home. These all can represent the context for today's real estate market. The developer may not be able to weather the financial difficulties of fewer sales in today's market. If technology is "silo-ed" or kept separate from knowledge of today's market, then the developer will probably miss the mark.

Typical of organizations, whether it is the organizational expression of a local church, or a government agency, one always finds evidence of "turf". In other words, certain folks only do certain things because "that's their job." Whereas a common concept in business today is the importance of cross-functional training, it is not common either in churches or in Government. Ironic isn't it?

The marketplace is far ahead of our stolid government and staid churches such that business sees the value of cross-functional training. It creates a larger context for the employee to operate within, and provides a diversity of experience that often lends itself to creative problem solving and innovation. Government on the other hand frequently finds its agencies and its personnel competing for any number of resources; human, financial and so on (think *Turf Wars*). Too many churches find themselves in similar shape with internal competition for responsibility and resources.

The larger the Government becomes the more of our "turf" they will demand to control. Power naturally collects more power. The influential seek to gain more influence. The wealthy seek to gain more wealth. Why is anyone surprised that Government seeks to govern more? As Government seeks to continue to grow its role in our everyday lives, it also seeks to concentrate power in fewer and fewer hands.

The continuing growth of Government at both the State and Federal level means that it is continuing to grow in its avaricious desire to control more. As "we the people" have allowed Government to manage a takeover of Auto Industry and Banking through bailouts, and with the bankrupt expansion of social services including unemployment benefits, the euphemistically termed health care "reform" we see a seemingly inexorable expansion of Federal power over so much more. When the Government talks about regulating compensation, then people need to wake up and see the "dictatorial" reality of Government.

As our Government seizes control of actual entities, and as it broadens the scope of its regulatory powers, we see the evidence of the directive and unhealthy impact of a Government that is dictating both utility and direction. With the financial-regulatory marriage of Big Business interests with LBGs, we are witnessing a massive erosion of the freedoms we once enjoyed.

What is ironic about it all is that while Big Business and Big Banking carry the influence to grab taxpayer resources to stuff their coffers, it is done with the statement that some companies are "too big to fail." Nevertheless, in the face of it all, there is no acknowledgement of the real engine that drives the economy. Small businesses, those with fewer than 50 employees, have more employees collectively than the large businesses receiving unwarranted Government subsidies. Yet, there is no bailout for the small business owner. The individual willing to risk it all for the pain and pleasure of self-directed value creation has been deemed unimportant by the "powers that be" in our esteemed halls of Governmen

Government has indirectly said the value of the small business owner begins and ends with the taxes they pay. The problem is that the taxes they pay are being stolen to prop up organizations that have performed poorly. Rather than forcing those institutions to pay the price for their decisions, "We the People" have allowed our Government to privatize the gains and socialize the losses. Thus adding insult to injury, their revenues are directed to Big Business while their own utility is derided, debased and otherwise delayed because of the "omniscience" of politicians who are more concerned with their own positional power.

Chapter Ten:
How they communicate

"I have learned that if one advances confidently in the direction of his dreams, and endeavors to live the life he has imagined, he will meet with a success unexpected in common hours."
~Henry David Thoreau

"Be happy. Talk happiness. Happiness calls out responsive gladness in others. There is enough sadness in the world without yours.... never doubt the excellence and permanence of what is yet to be. Join the great company of those who make the barren places of life fruitful with kindness.... Your success and happiness lie in you.... The great enduring realities are love and service.... Resolve to keep happy and your joy and you shall form an invincible host against difficulties."
~Helen Keller

Organisms are an integrated whole, and unless they are injured the various parts of the whole communicate efficiently and effectively. Organizations however, as was alluded to previously, have a tendency to break communication up across "silos" of information, where information has a tendency to bubble up, but it is rarely shared in a cross connective manner.

As an expressive community, churches ought to be inherently connective. Government, by its nature, has a tendency to divide responsibilities for various aspects of governance. There is some cross communication, but it is typically incidental in nature and a by-product of the realities created by the necessity that exists for inter-departmental, a.k.a. inter-agency, communication.

The purpose of communication between organisms and organizations is also very different. The organism "communicates" within itself and with other organisms in order to promote growth and healing. It communicates in a way that enables the entire body to be aware, so much so that it knows what is happening with each part, enabling it to care for itself.

Within an organization however, communication is not done for the purpose of creating awareness, nor is it even necessarily aware of other parts or aspects of itself. Rather, within an organization, there are many individual parts that comprise larger parts. Those larger parts define mechanisms that may or may not be used for moving the organization forward. Communication typically revolves around leverage and the means to accomplish some end or goal. If that end, or goal, cannot be met, then it is entirely possible that the parts so used may be removed from the "mechanism."

Government is inherently inefficient in its communication, and the larger the entity the less focused it is in its ability to communicate. A common misconception is that because churches must be organized as a corporation that they should also function like one. Because of this, they have a tendency to find themselves moving forward as an organization instead of being a community. The organic nature of the Church has a significant tendency to be lost in the organizational expression of individual churches or groups of churches (such as a synod or bishopric and the like). While legally churches are required to organize corporately for tax purposes, that legal requirement has also translated to how churches function as well.

Under President George W. Bush, the largest new government entity was created out of multiple agencies, known as the Department of Homeland Security (DHS). It was created to encourage inter-agency cooperation and sharing of information. Many critics of how the Government managed itself during the time prior to 11 September 2001 were the failures of multiple agencies to coordinate their anti-terrorism efforts with one another. One of the justifications for collapsing the organizational structure of multiple agencies into one super-agency, while still maintaining operational distinctiveness is that it was supposed to make communication more efficient.

Have you ever seen a fight where the little guy beats the absolute tar out of the bigger guy? Maybe you like martial arts movies like Blood Sport with Jean Claude Van Damme. Remember the scene where he is in the fight with a very large Chinese fighter and the guy almost takes Van Damme out? Well, in the end Van Damme's character Frank Dux takes out the big guy with speed, agility and determination proving that bigger is not always better.

What is desirable in communication? Most would agree that it is important to be clearly understood in communication. After all, the purpose of communication is to ensure that someone else unequivocally understands what you are trying to get across. Communication is at least a means to an end, though perhaps in some cases communication may in fact *be* the end.

Organisms communicate effectively

Certainly important concepts regarding communication have already been discussed such as the need for transparency. This concept is less about the "How" of communication and is more concerned with the quality of communication. Whereas the methodology of communication is concerned with the need for transparency, this points out the need for clarity.

Clarity. Being clear. No chance for being misunderstood or misinterpreted. Consider how easy it is for two people to misunderstand each other. However, within the body itself, signals are continually being sent to the brain and processed. For the person who is highly attuned to their body, they are able to understand not just that they are thirsty, but that they need to drink more water. The highly attuned person understands the difference between hunger and temptation.

Clarity in perception comes from making the effort to be efficient with what one says. In addition, an efficient communicator is not simply concerned with being clear. It comprises the ability to say what needs to be said in as few words as possible. This also reduces the likelihood that someone will misinterpret what is being said.

Effective communication means that it is unlikely that members of a group will misunderstand what leadership is saying if they are efficient. As a result, the group can execute tasks and move forward efficiently as well. Efficiency also can mean that there is an effective feedback mechanism. In the case of a body, or organism, the sense of touch enables someone to interact with their environment in a way that they can accomplish what they want.

For example, when driving, the individual is constantly unconsciously processing the information in their environment so that they can be sure to drive safely from point A to point B. Synthesizing complex sets of information is a critical skill to being able to drive safely. Everything from weather, to traffic signs and signals, to information available from the dashboard, along with the mirrors, and the steering wheel and so on, go into the constantly updating evaluation of the driving experience.

One piece of the environment that churches often fail miserably to work through is their ability and willingness to embrace diversity without trampling individuality. Sometimes people think, or define, diversity as being equivalent to alternative lifestyles. However, the diversity of personality, person and theology can make up just a few of the variables that a church organization needs to process. Many churches struggle with this…instead they have a tendency to create confusion through inconsistent messaging. They show an inability to communicate with folks with different "filters" and thus fail both organizationally and organically (as a church body) to meet the needs of their congregants.

Organizations confuse frequently

The larger the organization, the more distributed the group, the more difficult it is to effectively communicate to the entirety as a whole. In the case of Government, it is not just its size that causes its communication to be confusing; but also, also, its use of oxymorons' and double standards.

Government efficiency is itself an oxymoron. The Federal Government has demonstrated time and again that it is neither wise with taxpayer funds, nor efficient in its management of anything.

The reality is that even those things that the Federal Government has been tasked to do, such as National Defense and Border Security are inefficiently managed. Thus while on the one hand, the Government will state that illegal immigration is wrong and we need to protect ourselves from our foreign enemies, the Government fails to follow through on its Constitutionally directed responsibilities. That is both a double standard and an oxymoron.

A recent example of bureaucratic stupidity and Government inefficiency is the "Fast and Furious" initiative that ended with the murder of US Border Patrol Agent Brian Terry. A program supposedly designed to result in disarming the Mexican cartels, in fact, made it not only easy for them to gain access to weapons but also resulted in the death of American citizens. I will forgo flogging the proverbial dead horse in this case.

Churches organizationally fail to meet the bar as well. Consider the following oxymorons: benevolence committee, church building, administrative pastor ... and so on...

To define them, how does a benevolence committee demonstrate benevolence, in committee? What is it exactly that they ascertain or do? Most would assert that they determine who should receive benevolence and in what amount. Do you have a problem with that concept? While it is certainly an alluring idea that we need to be "responsible" with what has been given, there is no real scriptural support for the idea. A body of believers will have needs and resources. A group of believers normally responds to expressed need, if it is shared. Yet, many benevolence committees require an application, often including a financial statement, and one of the questions they ask is whether or not you have applied for public assistance ... need I go on?

Church building! Church building should be a verb and not a noun. The real Church is the body of believers within it, not the physical place where they meet. Most would accept this concept as true, yet we spend so much time and money creating buildings and sustaining buildings. There is no question that having buildings and space is very useful, but is it the best use of resources? The phrase is an oxymoron because the Church is not a building, though people talk about going to church all the time.

The concept of the Church being a body is why "administrative pastor" is also an oxymoron. Is it really reasonable to think that one can both administrate and pastor at the same time? How does one administrate, or dictate, what a group should or should not do, especially when that group is really organic in nature. We could rightfully argue that a group needs a leader, and that it is important for someone to be making decisions. Nevertheless, the counterpoint to that argument is that, at least as far as Christians are concerned, the head of the church is Jesus Christ, not the pastor, priest, or bishop. Perhaps the real reason that there is at times confusion in how religious organizations communicate is the result of leaders assuming a leadership role that is reserved for the Head of the Church, and that role is not meant for the head of a church.

When I was in eighth grade math class, I do not even recall the conversation but the class was laughing about something and I inadvertently sneezed really hard. So hard in fact, that I was unable to keep mucus from spilling all over my hand. I awkwardly stood up from my chair walked out of the classroom, and as I was leaving said "I'm leaving."

The entire class and teacher were shocked at the suddenness of it all. My teacher was instantly angry for my apparent upstaging of class. She sharply remarked something to the effect of where was I going and why. Upon my reply that I was only going to the bathroom and would be right back, she said you can take your books and head to the office. I was more upset about the potential embarrassment of being seen with mucus all over my hands than I was about being sent to the office. My reason for leaving was perfectly reasonable to me, but as no one understood my context for my statements and behavior, I was immediately punished for being unruly.

Was my teacher right for sending me to the office without listening to my reason for an abrupt departure? Was I wrong for making the mistake of not explaining myself more fully? As a child, I innocently made a mistake in how I communicated because of the social stress of the situation. In my mind, it was both forgivable and understandable. The principal and teacher both relented following my detailed explanation of what happened and did forgive me.

Should we be forgiving, disappointed, understanding, or outraged by the confusion wreaked on this country by pastors and politicians alike in the mistakes that they make? The question that must first be answered is whether they see, understand and admit the mistake. In most cases, pastors and politicians create confusion because they believe their statements to be infallibly true.

Intellectually they deny that they are infallible. Nevertheless, practically speaking, in terms of practice and manner of speaking they present their positions as infallibly correct.

Sometimes pastors of churches are co-opted for political reasons to make political statements to personally endorse candidates, petitions, movements, and so on. Unfortunately, sometimes the candidates are not representative of the value systems that the pastors and their congregations represent. For some who attend these churches, that sends a mixed message. That mixed message can create confusion.

The framers of the U.S. Constitution wrote in Article 3, Section 3, number 2, that there should not be "corruption of blood." Under English Common Law, when someone was convicted of a crime, their heirs were also considered "tainted" and therefore guilty by parentage. While the specific issue at hand in the Constitution is relating to treason, the legal concept presented is that just because someone is related does not mean that their rights should then be stripped from them following a family member's conviction.

We do not imprison the relatives of those who commit crimes unless they were accessories to the crimes themselves. Yet, moderates and progressives call it compassionate and "only right" to abort the child of rape. They state that allowing a child born out of rape to live is psychologically and physically cruel to the mother. These same LBG proponents, from moderate to extreme are typically anti-capital punishment. Restating the logic of their position, they believe that a rapist should be imprisoned, but that the child conceived as a result of that rape should be sentenced to death. Irrespective that abortion is scientifically linked to higher rates of breast cancer and causes Post-Abortion Stress Syndrome (PASS), LBG proponents of abortion are oxymoronically committed to an artificially structured concept of morality for murder that stands in direct opposition to the US Constitution and their own position on capital punishment.

The primary logic of pro-abortion proponents is that the womb, and therefore the fetus is the woman's body. Thus, it is the woman's choice. Yet, ironically, it is scientific fact that a baby upon conception has its own distinct body, and frequently its own blood type distinct from mommy's blood type. One might make the argument that the baby is "renting a womb." The LBG proponents would say that mommy has the right to evict the tenant. Yet, even a tenant behind on rent will be granted clemency by an eviction proceeding to enable a safe transition for a family in arrears on their rent. Who argues for the unborn child when it cannot yet speak for itself? Where is their right to a safe exit?

LBG proponents believe that abortion should be considered an amoral act, yet they criminalize the abuse of animals and they strive to protect endangered species such as whales. Why is it that the non-sentient members of Earth's fauna are more valuable than an unborn human child? Personhood has been arbitrarily stripped from the unborn because they are incapable of speaking in their defense. The unborn do not get many marches in the streets because they cannot be seen and they cannot be heard. Yet, worldwide in excess of 50 million unborn children lose their lives each year. Since Roe v Wade, scant months before I was born, the United States alone has already allowed the murder of nearly 50 million unborn.

Pastors and politicians alike have all created confusing and poorly constructed defenses for allowing the murder of the unborn. The many different things that line the value system of the LBG proponents in this regard are confusing, contradictory and all too often oxymoronic.

If organizations are confusing, and if churches are confusing, in their messages to members it is because of their frequent tendency to talk and operate with double standards. Their messages frequently appear arbitrary and only to the benefit of those making the immediate decision with little or no regard for the consequences. They appear to purposely obscure the reason and context for issues of concern. Is it any wonder then that "We the People" are angry with our Government and upset with our religious leaders?

Chapter Eleven:
Vision, ability to see beyond themselves

"Government is not reason; it is not eloquent; it is force. Like fire, it is a dangerous servant and a fearful master."
~George Washington

Organisms are typically wholly integrated and as a result, they have a tendency to be focused on the environment around them. They are attuned to the various parts of their whole, and as a result, they can afford to focus outside of themselves. Organizations are primarily focused on their various parts, and in attempting to ensure that those various parts function well, they do not typically have the time, the energy or the focus to look outside of themselves.

Some might argue and perhaps reasonably so that whether a group is organizational or organic in nature, that they must be able to focus both internally and externally. However, the emphasis in their focus and the manner in which they focus is a foundational and critical differentiator between them.

If you consider the general trend of most churches, the sad and misconstrued truth is that somehow programs equate to community. Many would argue and protest loudly saying "Not *MY* church! We are a wonderful community." However, if we set about wandering the halls of many American churches what we find is antithetical to the creation and sustainability of healthy community.

Our sanctuaries contain hundreds of people, facing the same direction and focusing on a stage. A community allows the parts of the whole to focus on each other, and to pay attention to what is going on around them. Most church organizations have great difficulty in creating community that interacts with the community in which they live. They expect people to come "in" to the church building, and that people can "plug in" to the various groups, which are actually in most cases programs.

Government is primarily focused internally because the nature of government is restraint. Government, when it acts, can only act to control, restrain, or remove. Former President Gerald Ford is credited with having said, "A government big enough to give you everything you want is a government big enough to take from you everything you have." Or to paraphrase another version of the quote, "Government cannot give you something that it has not already taken away from someone else."

The concept of direct taxation is barely 100 years old in this country. Prior to the establishment of the Internal Revenue Service (IRS) and direct taxation, the country gathered funding less directly from taxes on businesses, imports and exports, tariffs and so on. In the last 5 to 10 years, the LBG proponents have been putting a significant push on presenting taxation as a moral patriotic duty.

There is a direct attack on the financial resources of those who make "more than their fair share." This blatant class warfare is an unseemly presentation of a socialist ideal that is ruining American lives. This is the kind of classicism that seeks to permanently enslave the lower class through the enfeeblement of entitlement. Need a Government program for something? It is funded through excessive borrowing and heavy taxation on income.

What is the point? In order to run programs, whether it is a church or a Government agency, one cannot do so without having taken something from someone else. A community naturally and quite easily moves resources as needed, where needed and when needed. Government should not be in the business of meeting needs. The purpose and role of Government ought to be restrained in its expression to be solely concerned with providing for the safe expression of freedom in community. No more and no less.

Organisms focus outward on their clients (internal and external)

An organism does not need to have an external force determine how it should make use of its resources. The members of a community typically join together for mutual benefit and in most cases because they have similar goals and ideals. This concept is eminently expressed in the development of the thirteen original colonies that were themselves wholly different from any other and imbued with characteristics that attracted some and were consequently not attractive to others.

When one considers what focus means in this context, it is really not the simple definition of the word such as "to converge on or toward a central point of focus;" or "to concentrate attention or energy"[7]. Certainly, while it is true that the energies of a group will move towards a central theme or goal, that is also somewhat reductionist in nature. It is more accurate to see the focus of an organism as being able to anticipate, respond and meet the needs of its individual parts. Then, that organism will interact with others in concert, though with a broader set of alternatives. It will evaluate and anticipate what is happening in the general environment, and

---

[7] The American Heritage® Dictionary of the English Language, Fourth Edition copyright ©2000 by Houghton Mifflin Company. Updated in 2009. Published by Houghton Mifflin Company. All rights reserved.

then decide whether it should meet, ignore, or respond to the expressed needs of other organisms.

The individual parts of an organism comprise its internal members (a.k.a. congregants or constituents). The external organisms, or groups, with which an organism, or community interact may be comprised of individual parts or of groups of individuals that make up a community-at-large, whether formally organized or not.

There is no question that most churches will focus well on their internal members. However, it is their ability to "get outside" themselves that distinguishes whether they are operating as an organism (community) or as an organization. Unfortunately, many churches are focused on increasing the number of members so that they can "do more." The problem as a result, is that they have a tendency to be unable to consider the needs of those in the community or communities that they are in contact with, or find themselves within.

The larger an organization the more influence it wields. For example, consider Saddleback Church pastored by Rick Warren. Some might consider Saddleback Church's sponsoring of a Presidential "Forum" to be an undue imposition of the church into the political process. Others have suggested that it provided a venue to present the qualities of both candidates to the public-at-large. The reality is that it was simply a program that had very little to do with its role as the organizational expression of its community.

What did it have to do with? You should ask a member of their community - the answers will be all over the board. It is unlikely that there will be a unanimous answer. Instead, the answers will probably eventually distribute themselves into a series of similar answers. However, when it comes to meeting the "needs" of that community or the communities to which it is connected, what needs were met? Was there a need to provide a "soft" venue for both presidential candidates to "talk about themselves" and their campaigns? During the 2008 Presidential Campaign, did Saddleback and Rick Warren, do a disservice by excluding candidates from other parties such as Chuck Baldwin of the Constitution Party, Bob Barr of the Libertarian Party, Ralph Nader an Independent, and Cynthia McKinney of the Green Party?

On the flip side, consider this more generically. Many churches provide a multitude of programs for every age group. One church that I attended for almost 5 years had a newspaper with more than

185 groups that a person could participate in. Was that organizational or organic? How does one effectively integrate that many disparate pieces? Should one integrate those many pieces?

Unfortunately, many churches have a tendency to separate the different groups. While it is beneficial for folks to associate in smaller affinity groups, the problem comes when the integrated whole is neither integrated nor whole. The inability for many churches to reach outside of themselves in any coherent or effective manner is emblematic of their inability to meet their expressed goal of reaching the community "outside" their own. Certainly, one will find individuals that go out into the community and seek to meet needs, but the end result is always the same: bring individuals from outside inside so that they can serve the larger needs of the immediate community.

Some might suggest that this is an argument against proselytizing or seeking to introduce others to the faith, whatever that faith may be. However, that is shortsighted, inflammatory and missed the forest for a few specific trees. This is arguing against proselytizing for the purpose of growing the church organization so that it can sustain itself. The sustainability of a church ought to be found in its ability to equip, energize and motivate its members to meet the needs of the community-at-large. In so doing, the by-product will be growth. As growth occurs, it becomes a reasonable barometer to check whether or not the church is functioning properly.

However, growth does not, and should not, occur for its own sake, or more specifically simply so the organization can find itself growing in influence. The influence of a community within a community, or as a part of a group of communities, is better measured by that community's ability to interact positively with the other communities that it "lives with." Positive interaction means, "Seeking to meet the needs of those around it, as well as those of the group itself, rather than one or the other."

Many churches would argue that their focus is outward and not inward. Reality is found in the propagation of programs that exist, or are continued, to the denigration or dissimilation of the community itself. Most churches in America today grow through transfer growth, meaning people who already are "of the faith" choosing to associate with a different organization of believers. This should not be the primary fuel for the growth of individual church groups. Rather growth should come from interaction with the community-at-large. While some eschew proselytizing, evangelism should elicit the response of "the uninitiated" unbeliever. Folks hopping from one location to the next looking for some community to serve their needs make the same mistake. Rather than seeking to meet the needs of the community, they are thinking of joining, they look for a church that will serve their needs.

When it comes to our churches, religious and spiritual leaders need to cease demanding and start demonstrating real sacrifice. People respond in kind, and are capable of so much more, especially when they are ably and humbly led by those who have experienced the joy of true sacrifice.

I submit to you that the reason most churches struggle today is because they have not learned lessons of the social and spiritual realities behind sharing and demonstrating sacrifice. It is time for the shepherds of all spiritual organizations and institutions to return to a meaningful understanding of sacrifice. This means that each community should explore what that means for their immediate community, as well as what it means for their community-at-large. Failing to do so is an abject failure to recognize the true nature of the Church, locally and at-large. The current discussion in most churches has instead become a vapid and shallow exercise in "sustainability."

Organizations focus inward on the needs of themselves (programs)

Government ought to be primarily focused on the internal needs and aspects of the community, or communities, that it serves. However, whether it is through programs, initiatives, or agencies, Government seeks to sustain its own existence by extracting what it needs from its members (a.k.a. constituents). Unfortunately, many churches find themselves effectively doing the same thing. For example, it is not uncommon for many churches to lambast and otherwise berate their constituents to "give more" because if they do not give more they are "robbing God," or more manipulatively suggest that they are "missing out on the blessing." In this way, most churches fail to act as a nurturing organism and flop their way into their community as an organization instead.

While it is true that Government interacts with groups of all shapes and sizes, the focus has not shifted away from itself. Organizations move to benefit themselves and ensure their own continuity. It does not matter what kind of organization there is, as a business, as a church group, or a government entity, all organizations act and react, move and countermove, in order to benefit themselves. As a result, we can say with certainty that the nature of Government is naturally inwardly focused and self-interested, this is, after all the nature of organization.

The organism, while it seeks to benefit itself, is capable of seeking the benefit of those with whom it interacts. While there is intrinsic value in seeking mutually beneficial opportunities for interaction, organizations are not designed to have an outward focused. Nevertheless, the organism is capable of making transactions or moving in a manner that demonstrates something more than basic self-interest. The actions of an organism may be one directional and beneficial to another. Or, more simply, an organism is capable of sacrifice.

This is the most significant differentiator between an organism and an organization, and that is sacrifice. An organization will sacrifice its individual members in order to serve itself and save its programs. An organism will sacrifice itself in order to save other members regardless of programs. When one is considering the nature of a church versus the nature of government, sacrifice becomes a clarifying indicator of what church can be, and what a government should not be.

The question was phrased by John F. Kennedy (JFK) as "Ask not what your country can do for you. Instead, ask what you can do for your country." This is the penultimate definition of government versus church; organization versus organism. Many people love this quote, but few have seriously stopped to consider what the implications of this message are.

The implication is that Government needs to ask you to sacrifice. What are you asked to sacrifice? You may be asked to sacrifice your life if your profession is either Law Enforcement or Military service. In the most recent presidential campaign, it was suggested that paying taxes was a patriotic duty. To some this appeared to be an outrageous statement, but the reality is that this is the logical outgrowth of seizing the seemingly benign and patriotic statement of JFK.

The organism does not need to be manipulated into sacrifice with some sort of pseudo-guilt, nor will it seek to demand sacrifice from its members. Tragically, many churches ask their members, and even demand their members, sacrifice to the organization. This is church turned upside down and inside out. Church ought to be a focused community set on self-sacrificially giving of itself to its community, both internally and externally. Unfortunately, the question of stewardship becomes lost in the noise of the need to sustain the organizational expression of the church.

Have you ever heard of a "tithe march" or a "donation drive" or a "giving drive" or some sort of "capital campaign" where the church organization asks its members to "sacrificially give?" It would be more appropriate for the organizational expression of the church to seek as many ways as possible to give of itself to its community, and to the community-at-large. Successful church organizations intrinsically understand this concept and reap the rewards as a result. The one's that do not are seemingly always running "creative campaigns" and asking for "tithing testimonies" to persuade the members of their community to "just give a little more." Have you ever heard, "there are *<blank>* number of families in this church, and we only need *<blank>* number of dollars more each month in order to do *<blank>*." Listen to the words and one will usually find some program buried in the "to do *<blank>*."

Government will take everything you have if you let it. Currently our Government knows no limits or bounds on the demands that it is making on its citizens. If America were an actual woman, she would be the rape victim brutalized by a Government that takes what it wants, when it wants. Government is the rapist who turns to the victim and says, "You know you wanted it … You're getting exactly what you deserve."

Rapacious spending is made worse by the multiple bleeding ulcers of over-taxation cloaked with patriotic language. Wake up America! Sound the Alarm! The rape of America is being foisted by a Government running her headlong into full on bankruptcy while the vast majority of Americans are either duped or do not care any longer. If we fail to stand up for the rights we have been guaranteed, then we will eventually lose the ability to exercise any of them.

America the Beautiful is being taken advantage of in so many other ways as well. Our Bill of Rights is faring badly in an assault from both internal and external foes. They come from so many directions that it seems as though the attacks will never stop. Between the United Nations, foreign powers, the radical Islamic community that seeks the eradication of the United States and Israel, and our own Government, America is a gang-rape victim that is not being allowed to get up off the floor. Our defenses appear to be growing weaker. When a supposedly conservative Chief Justice of the Supreme Court of the United States of America (Chief Justice Roberts – July 2012) flips flops on the individual mandate, we know that Lady Liberty is being cut to ribbons. Lady Liberty is bleeding out on the steps of each branch of our Federal Government. Who will be the one(s) to take the knives out of their hands and stop the abuse?

The nature of government is control and restraint. It cannot operate without taking something from its members in order to sustain its own existence. Government cannot create value, and so it must extract value in order to function. Theoretically, Government provides greater freedom through a limited restriction of freedoms "endowed by our Creator" to each individual. The question becomes, what is an appropriate restriction of freedom? What is a necessary and due level of the expression and enjoyment of freedom?

The Founding Fathers defined those freedoms by restricting the reach of Federal Government through the content and context of the U.S. Constitution and the ensuing Bill of Rights. Unfortunately, today, there are many in our Government that seek to restrict those guaranteed freedoms in violation of our God-ordained and Constitutional rights. Why? One would suppose that it is to assuage their conscience and moral code (or immoral code, depending upon one's perspective). LBG proponents fervently believe that they know what is best for everyone. As a result, they actively and viciously seek to bend all citizens to the shape of their moral code. Their pseudo-moralism is just a mask to cover their true purpose – control. They seek to govern thinking, actions and words. Any denial of this is simply a naïve failure to see the LBG movement for what it is.

The LBG movement, through our Government is demanding that we sacrifice everything. Our Money. Our (Bill of) Rights. Our Children. Our Property. Our Thoughts. Our unborn children. Our future, collectively and individually is at stake. Will we respond as a victim of abuse and simply "try to survive," or will we gather our wits and our strength and say, "Enough is ENOUGH!" When we said, "No, stop it!" We meant it. So far, our Government and the Political Elite that feel entitled to run do not believe us. And why should they, we seem to be intent on letting the Political Elite continue running the country aground as though she were some whale to be beached and then plundered.

The right of our Government to demand sacrifice needs to be severely curtailed. Government, through the filter Bill of Rights, has the ability to ask for contribution – but nowhere does it provide a mechanism for such outrageous demand as we see today.

Chapter Twelve:
How they interact with other groups

"Do not wish to be anything but what you are,
and try to be that perfectly."
~St Francis De Sales

"A ship in harbor is safe, but that's not why ships are built."
~John Shedd

Association is powerful. In fact, it can be the determining factor in whether either individuals or groups succeed or fail. This is true in both short-term initiatives, as well as in terms of long-term survival. This is largely due to the fact that groups are made up of individuals. Individuals have their own particular flavor, and as a result each group of people whether they comprise a specific group or not will have a tendency to exhibit a specific "flavor."

While it is true that it is impossible to quantify, measure, reproduce, or detail specific distinctives that will always match all of the members of a group, it is also true that they will all have similar tendencies that give rise to the group itself. Some might call it genetics, some might call it culture, but it is the unique combination of genetics, culture, and the immediate environment that result in the reactions of individuals. The same can be said of groups, or organizations. Even groups are "hard-wired" with certain "genetic" tendencies that reflect their nature, representative beliefs of the group, and so on.

The Federal Government relates to the States and to the communities within those states, whether counties or cities or towns or villages. The United States is a vast collection of communities, and their interactions with each other are governed by the joint context of their state charters, or constitution, in relation to the U.S. Constitution. This is an example of the political context that gives some breadth and depth to the concept of group interaction.

Churches on the other hand may be entirely independent, or part of a denomination, a movement or an association that is larger than the individual church itself. Frequently, denominations, or groups of churches, associate with each other in order to combine and leverage resources. One of the positives with group associations, especially large groups, is their ability to accomplish more than any individual, or small group, can on their own.

Perhaps the most powerful demonstration of the ability of a nation to meet a challenge was created in the response of the United States to the onslaught of World War II. While there were many in America who did not want to see us go to war, once we were drawn in, the singular focus produced an amazing result. American manufacturing out-produced the rest of the world in every category. The entire nation endured a stiff rationing program that enabled the country to meet the significant demands of rapid production. Following the end of World War II, as the dominant manufacturing country in the world, we largely rebuilt or funded the rebuilding of war torn Europe and the Far East. When everything in-group or in-community aligns, the results are absolutely astounding.

While the immediate context of groups, or communities, within communities is reasonably obvious to the average observer, what is less obvious is the truth of the power of influence between these various communities. Consider the concept of association a bit differently. Think of the association of groups as a reflection of the statement "you are what you eat."

In terms of a group mentality, a group "eats" through association. In other words, healthy groups are healthy in part because they maintain healthy associations that are positive and contribute to the overall quality of the organization. When groups fall apart, or demonstrate unhealthy attributes, many times it can be directly related to the unhealthy associations they maintain. What they take in impacts the nature and flavor of the entire group, as well as the individual members themselves.

Organisms understand the power of proactively pursuing positive association

A true organism is purposeful in its pursuit of positive associations. Those who desire to have creative and positive relationships become the driving force within their communities for positive change and seek to create a positive atmosphere. This kind of positive drive towards the future is planned, it is not accidental. It is the proactive realization that in order to create a positive atmosphere, that the responsibility lies with the members of the group.

The power of positive association is similar to what happens when one gains proper nutrition and energy from power foods. Whether they are fruits high in their ORAC (Oxygen Radical Absorbent Capacity) number fighting off potentially cancer causing cells, or the muscle recovery power of protein, we know there are foods that inherently, and incredibly promote health and energy. Groups that behave organically understand that the same power can be found in the positive healthy relationships built in excellent association with other positive groups.

It has been said by a number of experts that our income is often reflective of the average of the incomes of the five people who influence us the most. That can be positive or negative. Who is influencing you? Whom do you influence?

Churches that experience explosive growth have typically keyed into something that we all desire. That is a sense of belonging, and communicating a sense that we can be more than we are currently. It is the sense of Hope that rises from the ashes of our daily experiences that reminds us, we are neither the sum of our experiences, nor are we the sum of our circumstances. This truth is audacious in scope to some, and it is the breathtaking wind of revelation blowing through the consciousness of each member that moves a church (or group) to be more than they thought possible.

How often have we wandered through the doors of a church and looked wistfully at the rows of people that appear to be so happy. We look around and poignantly feel our struggles, our faults and our failures. We walk out with a sinking heart thinking that our invisibility is exceeded only by our inability to taste the fruit of joyful relationship.

In our humanity, we are hardwired to seek relationship, and yet as we join in groups with others that we think are like-minded in faith, we find we are seemingly unable to find that real connection we so deeply desire. We chase it so many different ways, or we seek to numb our individual pain in any number of pursuits. What does this mean? Church that is divinely designed to be the place that creates and facilitates real connection instead falls so horrendously short that we find it impossible to connect with our fellow man. As we fail to connect in community, we find that our expression of faith and our sense of the Holy One lost its way as we wander away bleeding in our private pain and sorrow.

Our churches have lost the redemptive transformative power of transparent relationships that encourage others to join together in community, and to then associate with other positive communities. Instead of capturing that proactive power inherent in the pursuit of positive relationships, we instead find obstacles to relationship. Instead of capturing the hearts and minds of those in the group, our churches stumble into unfortunate and sometimes catastrophic pitfalls.

Organizations experience the negative impacts of reactive, unplanned association

How is it that Government and our churches unerringly find their way into the midst of negative association? It is largely due to the reactive nature of organizations. They are *always* running to catch up. Frequently legislation is written in reaction to something that has happened, and usually it is the result of something that has at least seemingly harmed someone. And, they craft their initiatives to attempt to prevent that harm from occurring again. This is the how and why rights and freedoms are frequently slashed and burned.

Two economists from UC Berkeley studied 11 recessions occurring post-World War II, and found a recurring theme in American legislative fiscal policy. The economy normally was in the midst of nascent recovery by the time Congress responded and passed anything that may have been potentially meaningful. Further, they discovered that policies enacted often were counterproductive to meaningful economic growth. Yet despite quality and reputable research from a variety of sources providing similar findings, Congress and Presidents tend to maneuver to score political points and interfere with useless policies that prolong recovery by making matters worse. ObamaCare stands a monumental example of just such a problem, and is set to explode like a tactical nuclear warhead ready to tear the heart out of the innovative engine of our economy.

The ad hoc and typically poorly conceived legislation is emblematic of the failure of Government to remain in the sandbox designed by the Founding Fathers. In our failing and ailing churches, initiatives and programs are started in the hopes that they will somehow respond to that which is desperately needed by "the people." The reality is that reactive initiatives, whether legislative or programmatic, fail to meet the needs of the people. Instead, they have a tendency to get in the way of the ability of people to explore real relationship in the honest freedom they unconsciously prefer.

Our churches and our Government are hooked on negative associations like those that are hooked on junk food or heroine. Whether it is an actual opiate or narcotic, or simply the addiction to flours, sugars and highly fatty foods, we intellectually understand that too much of it, sometimes any of it, is not healthy. In the same way, our churches are addicted to top-down leadership models and over-produced programs that prevent true community instead of enabling it.   As for Government, it is hooked on spending and taxes as though if they paused for even a millisecond, taxpayers might flee with their resources. The wealthiest taxpayers probably will flee.

The language of association in our modern society needs to be retooled so that we are able to step away from those things that are only a distraction from what is real. Government needs to set down the opium pipe of regulating virtue and thus limiting freedoms. Churches need to move away from the consuming fire of program and organization and reconnect with real relationship.

The tragic reality of organization is that it fails to create value. Instead, it can only receive what is given and then redistribute or consume those resources it has collected. This is why the bloated leech of American Polity needs to be torn, not just weaned, from the backs of those who create that value. This is why churches need to reconnect with their God-ordained designed purpose, engaging people in transparent community.

Chapter 13:
An Ethical Model to Begin Solving Our Problems

*"If you think you can do something, you have a much better chance
for success than if you wish you could."*
~Tom Kubistant

*"Our fatigue is often caused not by work, but by worry,
frustration and resentment."*
~ Dale Carnegie

We can argue that we are capable of solving our problems because we are smart enough, rich enough, technically advanced, or for whatever reason we want to hold to heavens. But, the answers do not lie with our capabilities or our abilities. The answers lie in depths of our mind. I do not mean this any kind of sloppy, insubstantial self-help, think positive way. Rather, we must come to understand the power of the beliefs that we hold to be true.

Why?

- Beliefs precede our thoughts.

- Thoughts precede our actions and our words.

- The results of our words and actions will only impact our beliefs if they are not strongly held.

- If our beliefs are strongly held. For example, the closer they relate to our personal identity, the less likely it is that they will change, regardless the outcomes.

A perfect example of strongly held beliefs is the ethical model, or ethical matrix, by which we make our decisions, specifically as it relates to our religious and political beliefs. As we stated at the beginning, our views of each impact the other. More specifically, our philosophy on governance is driven by our views of religion. Rather than calling it religion, we should call it what it is. Religion is what structures and drives our understanding of how the world works. If you claim to have no religious faith or belief system that is, in and of itself a belief structure. The following is a model of an ethical construct that demonstrates why churches and the Government cannot solve our problems.

Ethics: The Downward Spiral

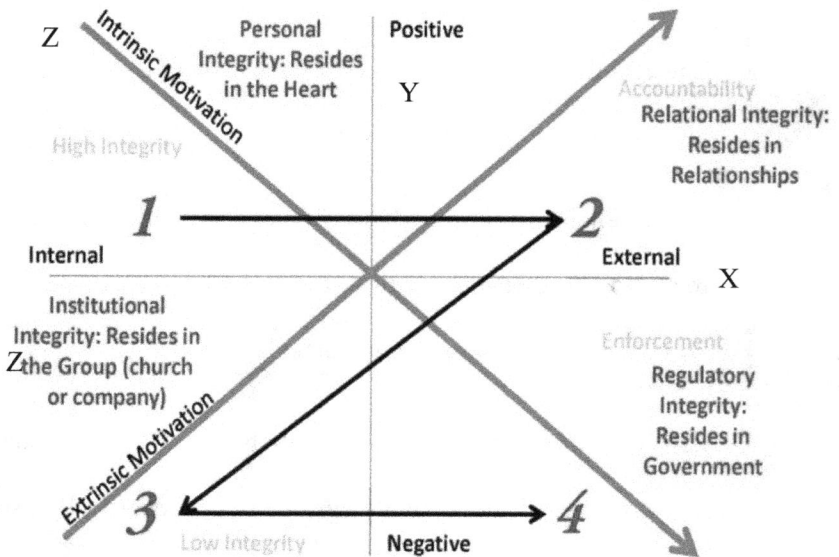

© 2006-2011 Benjamin Goss

While difficult to show here, this would be better presented in a three dimensional model, if you think of arrows connecting numbers One through Four as a spiral slide on a playground you can begin to see the representation more clearly.

The model is divided into four - three dimensional - quadrants named:

1. **High Integrity**: *Personal integrity*, your ability to make quality decisions, resides in your heart.

2. **Accountability**: *Relational integrity*, the quality of the relationships you maintain provides an external basis for decision-making.

3. **Low Integrity:** *Institutional Integrity*, the nature of the institutions, organizations or groups that have an understood set mores and values that drive decision making for them.

4. **Enforcement:** *Regulatory Integrity,* society through government has regulated what the minimum standards for ethics and decision-making.

The scale of measurement in the model is based on three axes. Each axis is better understood as plane, rather than a line:

X. The scale along this plane moves from internal to external, in terms of the driving force for providing the basis of ethics and quality decisions.

Y. The scale along this plane moves from negative to positive as one moves from the bottom of the model to the top. The connotation of negative versus positive relates to the nature of the relationships involved in providing the measure.

Z. The scale along this plane moves from high intrinsic - low extrinsic motivation in Quadrant One, to low intrinsic - high extrinsic motivation in Quadrant Four. Intrinsic motivation means that the motivation for quality decisions is already within the person making the decision. Extrinsic motivation strikes means that there is nothing necessarily within the person structuring decisions and ethics, rather it is being forced in some regulatory manner, whether through laws, or group expectations.

So how does this model demonstrate that churches and the Government cannot solve our problems? It is a visual guide that enables us to understand how the breakdown in ethics, or in the decision matrix, that people hold can result in the political, financial, relational and economic disasters that impact our lives, on every scale from personal to global. In my personal opinion, the more people that operate out of quadrants 1 and 2, the more freedom a society will enjoy. However, as the level of enforcement increases in quadrant 4, a people will become less and less free.

How free are we as a people? Answer this question, how much of one's daily life is governed by quadrant 4? A strong common ethic (in quadrants 1 and 2) is the foundational basis for freedom. Without a strong common ethic, we lose freedom of choice. When consequences increasingly come from quadrant 4, we consistently see the erosion of personal freedoms. When one powerful group feels that society must be forced to operate from a certain ethic, that group then uses quadrant 4 to force that ethic. Again, the loss of freedom ensues.

Consider the following statement: Ethics, ethical values, and a commonly held system of mores and norms provide a framework within which the individual functions. An individual's personal ethical system will always be in tension with the larger societal ethical system. When large groups have ethical systems that are dissonant, then there will be tension between and within those groups, especially in how they function.

Systems that crush, level, or flatten the "ethical spiral" do so by bringing an increasing amount of zones 1, 2, & 3 under the control of zone 4. This ultimately also becomes an erosive force weakening freedom. Our ability to express ourselves and pursue that which we desire is an expression of self-actualization or self-realization. The more that government intrudes on our ability to express ourselves, innovate and create value the less freedom we enjoy. Rather than allowing society's norms and mores to drive actions and consequences, proponents of the LBG philosophy continually strive to restrict not only our individual freedoms, but societal freedom as well. They seek to limit thought, speech and the expression of religious beliefs. For a more in-depth discussion of this model, please review Bonus Chapter #4, ***Proposing an Ethical Construct***.

Chapter 14:
Organism versus Organization,
is that really the question?

Yes and no. The contrast of organism and organization are illustrative in that it helps us to peel back the layers of presumption to examine what these groups should really look like. The argument about how Government and our churches ought to manage themselves is an oxymoronic conversation because it is an argument that reveals our perception of the purpose for both. If we agree as to purpose, then function will solve itself. However and unfortunately, we are polarized to the point that we passionately argue about everything from function, to purpose, to philosophy and even the theology behind them both.

When we consider the span of history with today, we find disturbing parallels between citizens of Rome and citizens of the United States today. It has been said that as long as the Emperor threw lavish parties, typically the sorts of "carnivals" and entertainment as one might find in the Coliseum, that the people of Rome cared not who was in power. There was an insatiable pursuit of entertainment that provided distraction from everyday woes and stresses. It is an established fact that this was the way of life in the first few centuries after Jesus Christ.

In the United States, there is a passive and apathetic approach to much of governance driven by the over-sexed, over-advertised, and supra-entertained masses. Sports, Media and Entertainment icons have been promoted to the status of near demigods such that the average person is frequently lost. How? They lose themselves in the pursuit of following the lives of celebrities such as Snooki, Tiger and Br-Angelina instead of taking responsibility for their own lives. While this may or may not be true of many, there are so many more that think their "way out" of downtrodden financial circumstances is to become a super star in one of those arenas. As a result, the American populace of today has replaced the arenas of the Coliseum and the Roman thirst for bloody entertainment with their own arenas, frequently filled with now-stylized violence and over-stimulating entertainment.

Am I suggesting that there is a problem with sports, media or entertainment? Yes and No. To borrow a phrase from one Greek philosopher "all things in moderation" to do otherwise is to waste one's opportunities in life. It's easy to shoot for the stars, sometimes we hit the moon, and sometimes we can't even seem to get off the ground... But, does that we mean we should not try? The energy, drive and motivation that it takes to move from apathetically passive to passionately driven all depend on the inertia of the individual.

How many times have you, or someone you know, talked of grandiose goals or seemingly impossible dreams only for you to find them haplessly playing games on Facebook? Getting started is ***sooo*** DANG HARD! For some of us simply getting through the day; juggling children, performing at work and the demands of bills feels like more than we can handle. If that sounds like you, then I salute you! You can do it! Every step you take may be the steps that move your inertia of hapless helplessness into the engine that drives your creative engine forward.

But, you and I, we must start today! Forget about selling a million dollar job, or landing that Vice President position. Let's start with making our current corner of the world better than it was when we woke up this morning. When you cannot seem to pry your eyelids open with toothpicks then that is when you are ready for breakthrough. When it feels like that first step out from under the covers will end your day before it begins, that's when human effort and superhuman will collide.

We have idolized the lives of the extraordinary such that the lives of the simply ordinary seem less than valuable. The truth is that it is the valuable lives of many ordinary folks that make the extraordinary have value. Without the ordinary, then where is the exercise of personal responsibility? Too many think that failing to be extraordinary means that life ceases to be anything worth mention.

We need to change our perspective of the extraordinary to be reflective of the regular efforts of those who simply contribute in a measured and consistent manner. The ability to contribute value every day, without the need for fanfare is perhaps more valuable. This is the engine on which every economy stands. It is the foundation on which every government stands. The willingness to stand forth for oneself and one's family while expecting only that which was promised in the exchange of time and service for the agreed upon value.

What is your story? Do you drive a bus? Are you a secretary in an office? Do you pound the pavement seeking to drum up business for yourself and your company? I have been a janitor, a teacher, youth pastor, Sunday school teacher, worship team vocalist, soloist, music director, political candidate, student, produce clerk, salesman, manager, multi-unit manager, server, project manager, consultant, business owner, and more. You are valuable to your company. You are valuable to your family. You are valuable to your community and your country. You matter. Each day you make a difference.

I am writing to call you and me to a higher plane of discourse. These essays have been written to provide a reasoned basis for the dialogue wherein we can find not only benefit but purpose as well. If then, the point is to illuminate, then the goal is discussion. The hope is that discussion will bring to the forefront the painful reality of the failures of both churches and Government to fulfill their appropriate and necessary roles.

Can one make the argument that perhaps Government should take an organic approach to governance? No, when Government grows it consumes more resources, and it restricts more freedoms. In order for Government to remain agile and healthy, it must not be allowed to grow beyond those boundaries already defined by our Federal Constitution.

Churches do need organization, but they need to ensure that the organizational aspects of function do not override the "body-organic" needs of their members. As has been previously suggested, the vast majority of churches have allowed the organizational aspects to sprawl to the point that the hearts and minds of people are no longer engaged. As churches organizationally focus in on program, people tune the ears of their hearts out.

Whether lost in the drive to "entertain" the masses or to subject the congregation to death by program, churches are absolutely failing to be the engaging, transformative force envisioned when the Church was originally "called out."

Our communities ought to be thriving engines of engaged people working together and creating value with Government standing in the background as an occasionally needed referee. Instead, our Government is bloated beyond any recognizable shape or proportion sucking value from the lifeblood of our communities faster than they can create it. Our failure to get Government under control means that "unsustainable" will be the wholesale collapse of our economy, and perhaps secondarily yet more tragically a total collapse of our society into a third-world cauldron of need, hatred and ruin. If our churches continue failing to engage their members with a "body-organic" understanding of how to function, then those churches will continue to dwindle and become an increasingly ineffective, un-impactful segment of our society.

The Living Church: Organism not Organization

Summarizing the Church as Organism; as a Christian, I believe that the Church is an organism. A living, breathing thing… why else is the Church referred to as the Body of Christ. I doubt that any living person can really fathom or explain the truth embedded in this statement. There are a great many illustrations and ideas that have been drawn from this statement, but it is not that purpose for which the statement is made here.

The Living Church is **NOT** an organization

The statement here is really directed at the fact that, at least here in America, the Living Church has become the church an organization. A legally defined entity that must meet certain definitions and criteria as an organization in order to be deemed a church, but even this begs a question. What is it about the legal organization that makes it a part of the organism the Body of Christ? I submit to you that it has nothing to do with it.

Trapped within the confines of our cultural and societal definitions of what church is, we are concerned that perhaps the

"American" expression of the Church has lost much of its vitality and the impact that it once had upon society in centuries past. What was it about the First Century church of Acts that forged it into the dominant religious entity of the Fifth Century?

For the Acts of the Twenty First Century to have meaning and impact, we must make the attempt to strip away twenty centuries of culture, tradition, and societal norms and attempt to derive what a Vital Living Church could be, perhaps even ought to be.

I don't know about you, but I am tired of living church done the way it is because it is just that – "it's done." Did you go to church last week? Have you visited church lately? What did you think about what the pastor, or those in attendance, had to say at church this weekend? We identify church as a place and not as the living breathing organism that it is... I appreciate a worship pastor I know who opens a service by making the statement, "Thank you for bringing the church into this room."

Where is the Living Church today?

It makes me wonder... is the American expression of the church today kind of like a leg left in one position so long that all feeling has left it? I am referring to feeling in terms of real compassion for people. Feeling in terms of a real deep felt emotional connection with Jesus Christ through the Holy Spirit. That kind of feeling seems to be sorely lacking in so many places…

There are some local church bodies that run dangerously close to being, or becoming, the kind of people that Paul warns Timothy about in 2 Timothy 3:5, those who "holding to a form of godliness, although they have denied its power…" Is the American Church, in general, so numb that it has simply ceased to be a real and influential force in our contemporary culture today? Or is it more accurate to say that we are numb to the extent that societal norms and pressures have more influence upon the Church Body?

Perhaps the lack of real and bloody persecution has left the real and Living Church in America struggling to "wake up." I say this as my own humble and limited experience, coupled with the interaction I've had with many other Christian brothers and sisters around the country, has left the impression that the American church in many instances has become more of a program driven, numbers obsessed, marketing and commercial giant than a community where the faithful encounter Jesus.

Plastic Christians are un-Living Church

Perhaps you are like me, and you are tired of plastic Christians that are incapable of being real about struggle or life or difficulty? There is a tiresome "cult of personality" of pastors that have raised the cry of "unity" to stifle the questions of the faithful. Since when was unity such an overriding standard, that we ceased to discuss intelligently how to live out and express our faith?

This is not to say that I do not believe in doctrinal distinctives or that doctrine should be somehow subservient to the whims and questions of the many. What I am saying is that just like the Bereans in Acts 17, we ought to be continually searching and reading the scriptures to be sure that what we are thinking and sharing with each other is Scripturally true and accurate. (Acts 17:11) Or, perhaps is it simply that many of us are either ill-equipped or simply unwilling to hold each other accountable in matters of spirituality?

If we are unwilling to interact intelligently with the Scriptures, to question, to search, and to learn then we are committing both intellectual suicide and spiritual suicide. We commit intellectual suicide because we are not "working" to understand and articulate our faith, which produces a weak and ineffective witness. We commit spiritual suicide because we are not approaching the Throne Room of Grace, and therefore actively seeking to become spiritually mature in our faith (Ephesians 4:12-15).

One of the greatest human philosophers in history, Socrates said the most important principle is to "Know thyself." For the Christian, this should be re-stated as we need to "Know Christ." In knowing Christ, we ought to be actively interacting with Scripture so that the Holy Spirit can prompt us towards true maturity in Christ Jesus. (Romans 12:1-2)

"For this reason also, since the day we heard of it, we have not ceased to pray for you and to ask that you may be filled with the knowledge of His will in all spiritual wisdom and understanding, so that you will walk in a manner worthy of the Lord, to please Him in all respects, bearing fruit in every good work and increasing in the knowledge of God; strengthened with all power, according to His glorious might, for the attaining of all steadfastness and patience, joyously giving thanks to the Father, who has qualified us to share in the inheritance of the saints in Light." (Colossians 1:9-12 NASB)

Resetting our Government

Anyone who has a shred of common sense and some exposure to what is happening in government at every level understands that the bloated beast is out of control. Inane comments such as that made by Congresswoman Pelosi regarding the Affordable Healthcare Act (AHA) typify the stupefying ridiculousness of regulation. "We need to pass it so we can find out what is in it." It is amazing that those in the Federal Government believe that "We the People" are that stupid. Unfortunately, while most of us are **not** that stupid, too many of us are either apathetically unaware or philosophically aligned with this philosophy to prevent the over-regulation, over-criminalization and over (fill in the blank ...) of our society.

THE SIMPLICITY RULE

If we are going to rejuvenate the economic engine of this great country, then we must begin by stripping away the largesse of excessive regulation. Too many politicians pass laws in order to create the appearance of meaningful contribution, but they end up over-regulating us with confusing, contradictory and over-complex laws. A good starting point would be to re-evaluate governance in this country and strip it down to the basics. Every aspect of

American law needs to be reduced. It is time to eliminate entire departments of Government and return control to "We the People." Government consumes the largest portion of the national gross domestic product (GDP) of any sector of our economy. Government should not be the largest employer in the nation.

Reshaping our Federal Government needs to be based upon returning Government to its Constitutional design. Government needs to end its involvement in so many aspects of our daily lives. Contrary to the beliefs of the LBG proponents, the Government does not know what is best for individuals and their communities. Government was never supposed to be involved in redistributing wealth, solving the problems of health and welfare, nor should it be entrusted with driving our educational systems. Everyone complains about how inflation drives some aspects of our economy harder than others do. Yet, on closer examination, we find that it is those areas that have the greatest amount of Governmental intrusion: education and healthcare to name just two that suffer the most inflation. Entire sections of our economy have been created through Governmental regulation such as environmental hazard and waste management, governed by the US Environmental Protection Agency (EPA).

WHAT SHOULD THE SIMPLICITY RULE LOOK LIKE?

The Simplicity Rule for Governance covering Federal legislation could be structured along lines similar to the following:

- No bill being presented for consideration should be any longer than 15 pages, single-spaced in a 12 point, Times New Roman font.

- Any bill being presented must be considered by a Congressional committee to examine and then vote on the Constitutionality of the measure.

- No external document may be referenced for inclusion within any new piece of legislation. The measure must stand on its own merits, and be succinctly designed and defined.

- No new agencies, departments, commissions or otherwise can be created. This shall not prevent the individual states for coordination of efforts they deem reasonable and appropriate.

- Any agency of Government that is not explicitly provided for by the U.S. Constitution shall be closed within 12 months. All facilities and personnel shall revert to the state wherein they are currently housed. All funding for these entities shall be returned in a pro-rata share back to the individual states for administration.

This is not a suggestion to slowly downsize government as though it is trying to quit cigarettes. This is a massive emergency intervention required before the patient dies from chronic addiction and overdose. "We the People" do not need the intrusion of Federal Government into every aspect of life. What we need is for Government to get out of our homes and our communities, and keep its focus where it belongs: protecting our borders, providing a safe economic environment for the growth and development of our nation, and to ensure that the Bill of Rights is properly interpreted and applied.

Government funding should be capped to a specific percentage of our national GDP. If the Federal Government were like any typical American, the credit card would have been taken away a LONG time ago. If we cannot afford it, then it is not necessary. Most American families with the exception of the political and financial elite understand what it means to make difficult economic decisions based on limited resources. Government should be held to a similar standard. If we fail to make the difficult decisions now, then it will be impossible to avoid a complete economic meltdown in the future. Spending that runs unabated runs the risk of permanently damaging the economic vitality and stability of our nation.

Am I suggesting that typical liberal sacred cows such as Medicare and Medicaid should be ended? Yes. Am I suggesting that the Department of Education should be closed? Yes. Am I suggesting that we can quit cold turkey – maybe ... If Government would stop taxing everything so heavily, then Americans would be able to freely contribute directly to needs in their communities as they see fit. States, counties and individual communities should be able to direct their resources to meet needs in their communities rather than suffering the dispersed value that happens when funds are siphoned through Washington D.C. first.

Is it as simple as immediately turning off federal funding? Probably not, so many people are so heavily addicted to federal sources of funds that an initial crisis would result from the abrupt end of so many programs and departments. However, there is an opportunity to drive growth and create value by titrating programs down and transitioning them to state control first, and review by the individual states for future funding.

Our funding for Government is an insatiable hunger that is continually driving to acquire more power, more control, and more funding. We need to gain the corporate drive to end the avaricious political corruption of our federal form of government. Everyone knows that it is out of control. But, no one is willing to step forward and say "Stop!" We must force Government back into the box that was designed to hold it, or it will consume us all and the USA will cease to be relevant in the world in any and every dimension that matters.

THE COMMON SENSE RULE

Coupled with the Simplicity Rule, there ought to also be a common sense rule. The Common Sense Rule might also be understood as a "Reasonable Man Standard." This would be a formalization of the very old common law concept. While it is most commonly applied in matters of tort law and criminal law, it should also be applied to how Congress establishes legislation. The concept in this case is as simple as the following:

- If a piece of legislation cannot be understood, or easily defined, by a "reasonable person with basic common sense" then the bill is too complex.

- If a piece of legislation cannot be equally applied to everyone, including members of Congress, then the bill should not be passed.

- If a piece of legislation exceeds the Constitutional mandate, as it can be easily explained to the average citizen, then the bill should not be passed [yes, this is similar to the simplicity rule].

It has been said that a failure to understand history dooms us to repeat it. If we refuse to learn from other countries that socialism is a now-failed experiment, we will repeat it – economic collapse, hyperinflation and all. If we refuse to learn that the pacifism and pandering such as Neville Chamberlain, PM in the years leading up to World War II only guarantees war, we will be facing nuclear terrorism because of our refusal to deal with the evil intentions of Iran, North Korea and Venezuela. If we refuse to learn from the lessons on fighting tyranny and protecting freedom as demonstrated by our Revolutionary Founders, we will cease to be free.

Nevertheless, if we are willing to remember the political savvy and the economic drive of our forefathers, then we will return our country to its federal principles, and republican (not GOP) values.

Then we will return to economic innovation and growth that gives hope and illuminates us all.

Returning to a Belief in American Exceptionalism

There are some in our society who decry the belief in American Exceptionalism. They act as though the patriotic fervor of those who love this nation is somehow disrespectful of other nations around the world. The LBG proponents, and others, who would espouse the denial of this view suggest we eschew our excellent heritage in abject blindness to facts. America is an exceptional nation *by design*. Because of the nature of how the Founding Fathers designed our government, the USA has become a destination for:

- Religiously independent thinkers – pursuing the freedom to follow God as they believe He leads them

- Entrepreneurially driven risk takers – ready to begin all manner of business and enterprises from agriculture, to industrial, economic, political, entertainment, and inventors

- The best and the brightest the world has to offer

- _____. You fill in the blank.

Early in American history, those who survived and thrived were those that had the strength, courage, will and adaptability to meet the challenges of their new nation. Who was it that came to America? We have gathered the best, strongest, brightest and most driven people from many nations. This is not to say that there are not brilliant people around the world – there are! The USA is exceptional because of who decides to come and pursue the dream of a better tomorrow for themselves, and their children's children. The Statue of Liberty raises a torch that represents hope and freedom to the rest of the world. Hope is why millions have come here over the past two centuries.

It is not "hope" in the campy, market-esque version blasted at voters in the 2008 presidential campaign. It is that optimistic belief that I can impact my destiny. I can shape my future. I can take the steps to improve not only my life, but also the life of those who follow after me. The inspirational, motivational, death defying, deep-in-your-gut belief that tomorrow will be better than today because I will not settle for anything less. These are the characteristics of our American forbears from every nation on earth.

The only reason American Exceptionalism falters or fails is because we allow it to do so. Who am I ... who are they ... who are you ... to suggest that America is anything less than exceptional? I will not. No my friend, I will not dance on the graves of so many by demeaning the very fiber of who we are!   We are exceptional, because of our heritage first, and second, because we choose to be exceptional each day.

As I close this out, I want you to know that I believe that we as individual Americans have the capacity to create a vibrant economy and take care of our families and our neighbors.   Historically, Americans have outperformed their European counter parts in both financial giving as well as in gifting their time and their talents. We do not need our Government to care for us. They do not do it well anyway. If Government would return our resources to us, then on our own and through our church communities we could meet the challenges we face in meaningful, productive ways.

Allow me to leave you with a brief poetic piece I wrote as I thought about what I was trying to say in this book …

It has been said that Freedom isn't Free.
　We all know that, but few of us live like it.
　　If we fail to maintain a high moral
　　　　and ethical standard as a society,
　　Then we will cease to be Free.
Our freedoms are directly linked
　　to our ability to govern ourselves …
　　　literally, morally and ethically.
True freedom that embraces all that Liberty has to offer
　Ensures that Government stays inside the box
　　　　　　　that was designed for it,
　　It steps outside the box we created for God
　　　　　and makes sure our experience of Him,
In community, never gets placed back inside anyone's box.
　When churches grow organically and relate thus, people thrive
　　When Government grows organically people lose freedoms,
　　　　　　　　and are oppressed
When churches grow organizationally instead of organically,
　　　　　people tend to die spiritually
When Government grows organizationally,
　　　　　people lose freedoms and are oppressed
Are these statements always true?
　　　Maybe yes, or perhaps not,
But it's true enough for us to consider what we do before it's
done.
I want eyes that see past the clothes someone is wearing today,
　　To really see the other person.
I need ears that hear past the automatic greeting
　　　　　someone gives me today.
I desire a heart that is compassionate
　　enough to encourage someone in the midst of whatever battle
　　　　　　they face today,
　　　　whether they share it with me or not.

!!! BONUS SECTION !!!

BONUS #1:

CASE STUDY:
Failure of the Subprime Loans Market

1.0   Introduction

There is no question today that the failure of the subprime loan market in America has shaken the global economy. While it is true that there were a series of ethics violations from the origination in lending the money to the bundling of subprime loans in mortgage-backed securities, it is also true that the context is wider than that of a mortgage broker processing a loan that should never have been presented to underwriting. The question that needs to be examined, is can we as a nation avoid this kind of market failure in the future? Was the failure simply a lack of moral integrity on the part of greedy mortgage brokers on Main Street and fat cat bankers on Wall Street, or is there more to it than that? The author submits the following discussion suggesting that systemic market failure of the subprime mortgage market was due, at least in part, to the societal failure to develop a broad-based culturally accepted value ethic.

2.0   Are individual ethical choices ever truly made in isolation?

Context is incredibly important in reading, but it is also important to understand in life. The failure to understand the context of what is being said, what is happening, or what is being done means that one cannot likely understand either the why or the entirety of what is being addressed. The challenges of the subprime market provide a series of instances which together created an avalanche of bad financial consequences culminating in a global world market that continues to struggle to recover on the eve of five years since the collapse began in early 2007. (New York Times, 2012)

Rules & Religion: *Wrecking America*

If there is a reasonable first cause to examine in the subprime loan mortgage debacle perhaps it ought to lay with the politics of money, more specifically the Community Reinvestment Act (CRA) first signed into law by the Carter Administration in 1977. (Dahl, et al, 2010, p. 1353) While the CRA was instituted, it was non-specific in terms of measurement and enforcement regarding how banks and lending institutions were to "help meet the credit needs of local communities" (Dahl, et al, 2010, p. 1353). However, in 1995 and 1998 in response to complaints by advocacy groups that the CRA was ineffective, the CRA was expanded with the addition of

> ... three specific performance tests – a lending test, an investment test, and a service test. The lending test ... is the most heavily weighted component in the overall rating and is the most widely scrutinized by community advocates (Apgar and Duda 2003). (Dahl, et al, 2010, 1354)

While it is clear that there is political support and regulatory oversight regarding the importance of providing credit in the subprime, low income market, the impact of the CRA on lending remains unclear. As well, banks could be denied the right to merge or acquire other banks if the CRA rating is too low. Therefore at a minimum, since 1995, there has been political and regulatory pressure to provide credit for the purchase of homes to as many people as possible, but especially to those in low income scenarios. (Dahl, 2010)

The failure of the subprime market, however, carries the weight of mistakes and issues with multiple issues in the value-supply chain for supplying mortgage funds. As the access to credit

© 2012 Butterfly Promotions, LLC   http://www.benjamingoss.com

was eased, mortgage brokers wrote increasingly risky notes. (Jennings, 2012, pp. 434 - 435) Credit became easier to access as investment bankers bundled mortgage backed securities, freeing up the ability of banks to lend even more resources. Mortgage brokers, warehouse lenders, major banks, and investment bankers all leveraged the system as fast as possible to such an extent that the entire system collapsed.

The choice of investment bankers to purchase bundled mortgage backed securities, or collateralized debt obligations (CDOs), in such a manner that they were designed to fail was a poor ethical and poor financial decision (Jennings, 2012, pp. 78 – 80). Mortgage brokers that created "ninja" loans, meaning "no income, no job and no assets" made poor ethical and poor financial decisions. Warehouse lenders and banks that participated in bundling loans, made poor financial and poor ethical decisions. While there were certainly instances of criminal activity seeking to take advantage of lax rules as easily available credit, those issues are merely symptomatic of the fact that the entire system was runaway unethically making poor decisions. It is simply not possible in today's economy for individual ethical lapses to occur in any real isolation. The global economy is too interconnected.

3.0   Do incentives to lenders impact loans offered to borrowers?

When considering the question, do incentives matter in the types of loan packages offered, the answer is a resounding yes. What incentive is more important and exciting than continued growth and prosperity? The kind that resulted in what Kal Elsayed essentially called easy money. "We made so much money, you couldn't believe it. And you did not have to do anything. You just had to show up" (Jennings, 2012, p. 434). Gil Sandler (2007) writes:

> By failing to impose realistic underwriting criteria on regulated lenders, while continuing to reduce rates, US regulators allowed legions of untrained, often unethical, commission-hungry mortgage brokers to exploit middle and lower-income consumers in the guise of helping them move up the ownership ladder. One plausible theory is that monetary and regulatory policy sought to raise the asset values of lower and middle-class homeowners while the economic boom was aiding upper-income Americans with top-tier tax cuts and soaring stock market gains. Real estate appreciation may have become a partial substitute for the absence of real wage income gains. (p. 4)

Some of the easy money was made available through "off-balance sheet transactions," called "structured investment vehicles (SIV)" which allowed banks to regain liquidity to continue lending (Sandler, 2007, p. 6).

Easy money, easy credit, and a manner in which to regain liquidity all contributed to the failure of the subprime market. Tom Bengtson (2011) bemoaned the reaction of the US Congress in its attempt to regulate mortgage steering for banking compensation (p. 4). Bengtson (2011) described the issues relating to compensation and the subprime loan mess as follows:

> Many so-called "mortgage professionals" who worked everywhere other than bank misled consumers in the

head real estate era of 2004-2007. These glorified scam-artists steered trusting customers into expensive mortgages – exotic products with fat commissions. They didn't care if the mortgage suited the borrower. (p. 4)

Thus, there is no question that incentives, including the most powerful, that of compensation, impacts the types of instruments that are offered to consumers.

4.0   The Role of Subprime Mortgages in the Market

Turano (2006) defined subprime loans as being given to borrowers who:

- …represent a higher level of risk with respect to standard … underwriting guidelines.
- … [have] poor credit history (previous credit problems);
- … [are] asking for high Loan-to-Value (LTV) mortgages;
- … [come to the table] with a high Debt to Income ratio;
- … cannot document all of the [required] underwriting … information. (para 5)

But knowing how subprime loans were defined prior to market collapse is not definitive in terms of the place that these types of loans should play in the market. Due to the significant risks involved in underwriting loans in this market, the lender needs to be prepared for significantly higher costs and loss. (Turano, 2006)

Since the failure of the subprime mortgage market, there is little if any role for the subprime loan in today's restricted credit environment. Clarence Rose (2011) writes:

> In today's home mortgage environment, mortgage lenders are being very careful and selective in the loan underwriting process in order to avoid additional mortgage delinquencies and foreclosures, and most institutional buyers of mortgage-backed securities are demanding and limiting purchases to high quality mortgage loans. As a result, mortgage lending institutions have severely limited new mortgage loans to only the most financially qualified mortgage loan applicants …. If the mortgage loan applicant does not meet the minimum financial requirements, there are no magical techniques or easy solutions to qualifying for a home mortgage at the best available rate or even at a higher rate. The best that can be done from a personal financial planning perspective is to take the appropriate action to correct any shortfalls as soon as possible in order to meet the mortgage loan requirements. (pp. 72 & 74)

In other words, the simplest explanation is that the subprime lending market does not really exist any longer. While it is true that if a borrower is capable of putting 20% down on the purchase of a new home, if their score does not exceed 620, the loan will probably not be underwritten (Rose, 2011, pp. 73 – 75). This is far in excess of the textbook definition for subprime lending, meaning a FICO credit score ceiling of 570. (Jennings, 2012, p. 434) The market no longer resembles anything that existed pre-collapse 2007. In essence it no longer exists as it collapsed from top to bottom.

5.0   Analysis of Systemic Effects of the Subprime Market

Considering that the global economy continues to struggle in the wake of the subprime market collapse indicates the extent to which CDOs penetrated. The failure of the market in 2007 has resulted in the loss of millions of jobs since that time, domestically and abroad. There still has been no sustained and viable recovery. The New York Times (2012) reported that gross domestic product grew at an anemic 1.3% in 2Q2011, far below what was originally projected (para. 7).

As to why the failure occurred, Joseph Gilbert (2011) suggests the following parties:

1. Borrowers, who may or may not have lied to lenders in their applications;

2. Mortgage brokers and lenders, who may or may not have asked the right questions or enough of the right questions or checked on the answers to these questions to justify the loans that they made;

3. Securitizers (institutions, including commercial banks and investment banks) that combine individual mortgage loans into bundles, divide the bundles into tranches, and sell the resulting collateralized mortgage obligations to investors;

4. Rating agencies that somehow managed to turn subprime mortgages into prime investments by giving a much higher rating to the collateralized

mortgage obligation than the individual mortgages might achieve; and

5. Investors who purchased these instruments without really knowing what they were buying. (p. 91)

In terms of defining the stakeholders involved, the list would need to be extended to AIG who insured a large bulk of the losses in the securities markets. Finally, the US Government and the US taxpayer become stakeholders in the wake of massive bailouts. Then as financial losses rippled across the globe, one finds that both foreign governments and foreign investors purchased badly structured CDOs. Thus, limiting a discussion of stakeholders to those who deal with borrower directly artificially restricts the scope of the economic impacts of the CDO market failure. (Jennings, 2012, pp. 78 – 82, 434 – 436 and Gilbert, 2011, pp. 87 - 91)

6.0   Conclusion

Can this kind of global recession be avoided in the world? Very few would assert that it is another credit crisis, or massive market failure resulting therefrom that would produce another failure. However, when one considers that the heady days of highly leveraged growth in the 1920's, one cannot fail to see the echoes in the Subprime CDO Market collapse less than 90 years later. Only a few generations removed from the Great Depression, is it reasonable to posit that sound ethics would enable a nation to avoid market collapse? Perhaps ... the best conclusion to this thought line was penned by Joseph Gilbert (2011), it is not simply a matter of ethics, but we would be foolish to ignore how it is related. He writes:

Can we then say that the subprime mortgage mess described at the beginning of this article, with all of its attendant harms and negative consequences, has been caused by the unethical or immoral actions of some individuals? At least in part, yes. Otherwise, we have to maintain that foreseeable harms resulting from the decisions or actions of individuals are somehow disconnected from those decisions or actions. It may well be that no single broker, or loan officer, or member of a loan committee, or executive who approved inappropriate product lines, thought that he or she was going to cause anything like the mess that has resulted, and in fact, no single individual did cause the subprime lending mess. However, the aggregated decisions and actions of many individuals did cause the mess. It did not simply fall from the sky or magically appear at the confluence of several streams of actions. (Gilbert, 2012, p. 104)

7.0   References

---. (2012, January 12). Economic Crisis and Market Upheaval. *The New York Times.* Retrieved 12 January 2012, from http://topics.nytimes.com/top/reference/timestopics/subjects/c/credi t_crisis/index.html?offset=0&s=newest .

Bengtson, T. (2011). TILA & compensation. *North Western Financial Review, 196*(15), 4.

Dahl, D., Evanoff, D. D., & Spivey, M. F. (2010). The Community Reinvestment Act and Targeted Mortgage Lending. *Journal Of Money, Credit & Banking, 42*(7), 1351-1372.

DeZube, D. (1998). The stress of subprime servicing. *Mortgage Banking, 59*(1), 102-112. Retrieved from http://search.proquest.com/docview/234936533?accountid=28180

Gartenberg, C. M. (2011). *Essays on firm scope and incentives.* Harvard University). *ProQuest Dissertations and Theses,* Retrieved from http://search.proquest.com/docview/889089678?accountid=28180

Gilbert, J. (2011). Moral Duties in Business and Their Societal Impacts: The Case of the Subprime Lending Mess. *Business & Society Review (00453609), 116*(1), 87-107.

Loyd, L. (2008, Sep 22). Lenders lost moorings, some say. *McClatchy - Tribune News Service,* pp. n/a. Retrieved from http://search.proquest.com/docview/456824012?accountid=28180

LOUTSKINA, E., & STRAHAN, P. E. (2009). Securitization and the Declining Impact of Bank Finance on Loan Supply: Evidence from Mortgage Originations. *Journal Of Finance, 64*(2), 861-889. doi:10.1111/j.1540-6261.2009.01451.x

Rose, C. C. (2011). Qualifying for a Home Mortgage in Today's Mortgage Environment. *Journal Of Financial Service Professionals, 65*(2), 70-76.

Sandler, G. (2007). Aggressive Mortgage Lending and the Housing Market: The Economic Impact of Minor Miscalculations. *Real Estate Finance (Aspen Publishers Inc.), 24*(4), 3-9.

Turano, E. (2006). Subprime mortgage lending: Recognising its potential and managing its risks. *Housing Finance International, 21*(1), 37-42. Retrieved from http://search.proquest.com/docview/216202331?accountid=28180

BONUS #2:
Goldman Sachs: Shades of Grey

ABSTRACT (doctoral research essay)

The intermingling of issues surrounding the bailout of Goldman Sachs and AIG as it relates to the complete disintegration of the collateralized debt obligations (CDO) market is a tale of financial double dealing and economically disastrous woes. Goldman Sachs admitted that it behaved unethically in its representation of the CDO market wherein it created a financial maelstrom that ended up swindling tax payers out of billions of dollars thus effectively privatizing the profits, and socializing the company's losses all while providing no real benefit to the victims of the subprime mortgage backed securities debacle, nor to US taxpayers. The fact that Congressional hearings were held and that Goldman Sachs admits that mistakes were made, but that no real changes have been effected at Goldman Sachs is a sad commentary on the ability of the SEC to regulate Wall Street. The unfortunate reality is that Wall Street and the US Federal Government under two separate administrations have bilked the American Taxpayer out of billions of dollars to stabilize companies that perhaps should never have been subsidized in the first place. Why? It is because Goldman Sachs did not pay back its clients for all of the losses sustained under the CDO disaster. The only moral certainty is that nothing ethical or moral has transpired for many of the clients of Goldman Sachs in the midst of their losses.

Table of Contents

GOLDMAN SACHS: SHADES OF GRAY

1.0   Introduction

The question that needs to be examined is whether or not the impacts on Goldman Sachs for its role in the collapse of the Collateralized Debt Obligations (CDOs) market were sufficient. The fact that Goldman Sachs and AIG were able to successfully maneuver a bailout with taxpayer dollars, while not being required to pay back 100% of client's losses due to the failure of the CDO market all in the wake of Sarbanes-Oxley (SOX) begs the question; Does SOX, or more generically, government regulation of marketplace serve a useful purpose? The final question that ought to be addressed is the matter of company bailouts and industry bailouts: should they or should they not be allowed to continue?

There are multiple threads of consideration involved in the questions of effective governance of business and good business ethics. The issues that swirl around these issues are more complex than questioning if the actions of Goldman Sachs were both legal and ethical. The role of government in its regulation of the markets is called into question. The involvement of Goldman Sachs executives and political figures, a number of whom are former Goldman Sachs employees, highlights the internecine nature of high level politics and über-large business. If the Occupy Wall Street movement could articulate a coherent point of view, the issues involved in the Goldman Sachs-AIG debacles would provide adequate fodder.

2.0   Goldman Sachs: A History of Questionable Corporate Ethics

Goldman Sachs is a very large investment firm with over $1 trillion in assets as of May 2010 and with a very long history having been founded in 1869 (Jennings, 2012, pp. 73 & 82). Unfortunately, the firm's recent issues with financial market collapse are not new. In addition to contributing to the CDO market collapse in 2008, the firm developed a strategy called "layering" in the 1920's that contributed to the 1929 market collapse (Jennings, 2012, p. 73). A series of contemporary business practices on the part of Goldman Sachs are questionable described by Marianne Jennings as follows (Jennings 2012):

1. Standard underwriting practice requiring three years of profitability was reduced by Goldman during the hot internet IPO days of the 1990's to only one quarter, and companies were provided with underwriting even if profitability was not projected for some time. (p. 75)

2. Goldman "engaged in laddering," a process of utilizing preferred clients to artificially synthesize demand and pricing. (p. 75)

3. Goldman positioned itself short on the sale of "mortgage-backed securities such as CDO's" even while continuing to sell mortgage-backed securities to clients. (p. 76)

4. Goldman positioned itself as the foundation for multiple layers of securities trading resulting in massive leveraging, over exposing the firm to risk, and in 2008 received a $10 billion dollar

bailout of taxpayer funds in order to prevent failure. (p. 76)

5. Goldman's trading huddles were markedly different from those of other trading firms in that they excluded analysts covered under SEC regulations, and offered tips and advice to their own traders and preferred clients that varied from that which was published by the firm. (p. 78)

6. The Auction-Rate Market was developed by multiple firms and created a demand for certain securities wherein the clients trading were unaware of the trading firms' involvement in artificially driving the demand. Goldman Sachs withdrew from this market, caused this entire segment of the market to collapse, and then failed to make large institutional investors whole. (p. 78)

7. The ABACUS, a CDO deal put together by Fabrice Tourre had multiple questionable aspects to the deal (pp. 78 – 81):

   a. The fact that Goldman took "contra-client positions" on stocks, meaning that Goldman itself was trading in opposition to recommendations it was making to clients (pp. 78 – 80).

   b. It would appear that Goldman through Fabrice Tourre positioned itself to profit from a deal that was predicated on failure, that being CDO's (pp. 79 – 80).

    c. Experts have stated that conflicts of interest are a matter of fact in trading and that Goldman managed these conflicts through memos and fine print disclosures (p. 80).

    d. Goldman used the "qualified" and "sophisticated" status of its clients to provide an additional layer of plausible deniability, though the lack of transparency in Goldman's trading positions is hard to justify from a fiduciary standpoint (p. 80).

    e. Goldman used ACA Management in selecting the mortgage pool, and as well utilized AIG to insure the CDO's to provide arm's length distance from issues with the funds. Further, the use of ACA and AIG provided an additional layer of pseudo-security to investors that masked the true purpose of the program – the eventual failure of the CDO's ensuring profitability to Goldman and its people, of whom John Paulson appears to be foremost. (pp. 79 – 80)

8. In 2009, Goldman had a record year of profits wherein the bonus pool alone was estimated at more than $20 billion dollars. Yet, in 2010 following Goldman's failure to notify clients of pending action from the SEC, Goldman was formally charged by the SEC and suffered a more than $21 billion loss in value. While

204 | P a g e   Rules & Religion: *Wrecking America*

Goldman agreed to pay more than "\$550 million
in penalties and client reimbursements," losses
sustained by clients were still estimated to have
been roughly \$1 billion. (p. 82)

3.0   The question of legality set aside, is it ethical and is it
moral?

The Merriam-Webster Dictionary, online, defines moral in an
ethical context as "of or relating to principles of right and
wrong in behavior" (2012). This basic definition of moral
coincides well with a Kantian view of ethics wherein one
applies the "universal law standard" as a "Categorical
Imperative" (Jennings, 2012, p. 13). Because there are multiple
ethical theories, and because these conflict somewhat in their
application, it is thus important for the individual to make a
choice as to an ethical system. A failure to choose a specific
"moral compass" if you will for making complex ethical
decisions means that while may believe they are an ethical
individual, they will in fact become a *de facto* moral relativist
adjusting the theories and applications of ethical structures to
justify their own desired outcome. Moreover, in the words of
Alexander Hamilton, "those who stand for nothing will fall for
anything." In this particular case, those who do not have an
established, prepared ethical system, will end up making poor
decisions both morally and ethically speaking.

In applying Kant's Imperative to the series of ethically
questionable actions taken by Goldman Sachs, an overall
pattern emerges, that is disturbing and helps to elicit why the
company paid dearly in terms of penalties and client
reimbursements. The practices described in numbers 1 through

© 2012 Butterfly Promotions, LLC   http://www.benjamingoss.com

5, and number 7, all have one particular thread in common: they are all a demonstration of a lack of transparency on the part of Goldman Sachs. There is no question that Goldman Sachs needs to do what it can to maintain profitability.

However, what each of these actions described are actions that were designed to create advantageous trading positions for Goldman, at least in part, by not providing all of the information that might have a bearing on a client's decision to invest or divest. Anecdotal wisdom tells us that a failure to tell the whole truth is still a lie. In light of Kant's Imperative, it is impossible to justify the lack of transparency on the part of Goldman to disclose its positions and opinions to its clients, regardless the level of sophistication of the qualified investor.

Number 6 is a complex series of ethical failures that combines a failure in transparency with the outright deception caused by involving reputable third parties. What is most telling about the ABACUS trade, is that Fabrice Tourre appears to have been guilty of simply "relabeling" the indiscretion of the trade by stating his belief that he was providing a service to the US Consumer by making "capital markets more efficient and ultimately provide the US consumer with more efficient ways to leverage and finance himself" (Jennings, 2012, p. 80). That Mr. Tourre understood the irony and conflict of the statement bears out in his following rationalization "...so there is a humble, noble and ethical reason for my job ;) amazing how good I am in convincing myself!!!" (Jennings, 2012, p. 80). The irony of it is that he even recognizes that he is rationalizing his actions.

Number 8 is a failure in that not only does the failure to make client's whole following their losses, it is the failure of Goldman to return to its tradition of making client's whole when their reputation is at stake. It would appear that the firm ceased operating with what would be more of a Kantian perspective of ethics, to a morally relativistic approach, wherein the chief value is the profitability of the company. There is an additional problem with the change in the practiced ethical system at Goldman Sachs that is the concept of long term versus short-term gains. Moral Relativism cannot provide long-term profitability because it is willing to sacrifice the fiduciary responsibility to the individual client in favor of the short-term profitability of the firm. Had Goldman been willing to maintain the Kantian-esque approach to making clients whole, it is possible that the importance of managing the public's perception of compensation might not have been necessary.

4.0   The Ripple Effect of Goldman Sachs Strategies

Goldman Sachs' ethical failures have ultimately impacted every corner of the American economy, and as well it has had an impact on the global economy. One reason for the impact is that Goldman Sachs has traditionally been a large pivotal and powerful player in financial markets not only nationally, but globally as well. However, it is also because Goldman Sachs was merely one bank of many that were engaged in the selling the same securities instruments, mortgage backed securities. This is evidenced by the powerful deleterious effects the failure of the CDO market has had on the entire US economy and by extension the world economy as well.

The New York Times released an article 12 January 2012 that summarizes the current "economic crisis and market upheavals" (2012). The Times (2012) writes:

> A housing boom in America and a number of European countries was followed by a bust and then a market tailspin that created the greatest financial crisis since the Great Depression .... *[Financial bailouts were initiated]* But while financial Armageddon was avoided, the crisis spread around the globe, toppling banks across Europe and driving countries from Iceland to Pakistan to seek emergency aid from the International Monetary Fund. A vicious circle of tightening credit, reduced demand and rapid job cuts took hold, and the world fell into recession. (paras 15 & 18)

The comprehensive, though brief review by the New York Times (2012), relates that the roots of the current crisis began with the Dot.Com boom and bust of the late 1990's. It was during this era, in conjunction with the Community Reinvestment Act (CRA) that resulted in a great deal of political pressure combined with economic opportunity to provide subprime loans. The industry, backed by the availability of easy credit resulted in a number of pressures that resulted in the housing boom and bust that culminated in the 2007 failures of the mortgage backed securities markets. Following the housing bust and the collapse of the CDO markets, there has been a global rise in unemployment and economic markets contracting or failing as credit became less and less available. In essence, there is no part of the global economy that has not been affected by the failure of the CDO market. This failure became the global catalyst for global recession. (New York Times, 2012)

5.0   The Goldman Sachs' Culture

There are three critical components to the Goldman Sachs culture as described by Marianne Jennings (2012): "One is 'long-term greedy,' which Goldman executives translate to mean "don't kill the marketplace." [2] The other mantra is "Filthy rich by forty" ... [and 3] "toes-to-the-line" activities and issues (pp. 76 – 77). It would seem that there is a conflict between an Adam Smith-ian ethic which describes the pursuit of self-interest in such a manner that long term objectives can be met (i.e. "long-term greedy) and a Hobbesian view of ethics which suggests that self-interest can be excessive (i.e. "filthy rich by forty") (Jennings, 2012, pp. 12-13, 76-77). It would appear that the penchant for self-interest fell too heavily on the interests of Goldman and its employees, without enough of a balance concerning the need for long-term sustainability.

The fact that the SEC sued Goldman civilly, rather than pursuing the firm for criminal charges is sufficient evidence to support that while Goldman walked a very thin line, it would appear that they did not violate the letter of the law, though in light of penalties and reimbursements Goldman violated the intent and spirit of the law. Jennings (2012) quotes "Eric Danallo, a former deputy New York Attorney General, [who] argues that 'the spirit of the law should control conduct and not a strained interpretation'" (p. 78).

As an investment banking firm, people at multiple levels of Goldman Sachs expressed that they understand their role to be that of raising capital. From Fabrice Tourre talking about leverage, to Goldman CEO Lloyd Blankfein talking about being a "banker 'doing God's work'" that underlying theme is presented as the firm's raison d'etre (Jennings, 2012, pp. 80 – 81). However, the firm's reason for being was in direct contravention to the positions it took concerning both internet stocks and the CDO market, so that in ensuring that Goldman profited it was also operating to the detriment of its clients.

6.0   Goldman's CDO plays, were they honest speculation or stacking the deck?

The question is relatively academic as evidenced by the fact that Goldman Sachs paid out over "$550 million in penalties and client reimbursements" (Jennings, 2012, p. 82). Jennings (2012) writes about the game of business being sometimes akin to that of playing poker, wherein the players play with the understanding that each ought to protect his own interests (p. 50). If Goldman merely took positions in the market, and did not market or talk about positions on stocks or funds that it was trading itself, then it would reasonable to suggest that the firm was not cheating. However, the firm designed its operations with the intent of operating in dichotomous, nearly schizophrenic nature in how it separated its regulated equity research analysts from "trading huddles" with the firm's traders (Jennings, 2012, p. 78). In effect, Goldman created plausible deniability in terms of criminal culpability, but was sufficiently duplicitous in its dealings to be nailed with heavy civil fines.

In the case of the ABACUS deal, Goldman through its employee Torre on behalf of Goldman and John Paulson created a fund that was designed to be intentionally weak. As a result, the deck, as it were, was stacked for failure from the start. While it would appear that any sophisticated investor ought to be able to examine the structure and composition of a deal to understand the inherent risk, Goldman structured the deal with the enhanced perception of using ACA Management to pool the CDO's, and by using AIG to insure the transactions. As a result, the perception is that Goldman was being intentionally deceptive rather than simply shrewd in its dealings with investors.

7.0   Ethical Failures Result in No Material Changes at Goldman Sachs

> Howard Chen, a banking analyst, issued these observations on the Goldman settlement: (1) He observed that there would be no management changes at Goldman; and (2) "We do not anticipate any material long-term impact to the firm's client franchise." (Jennings, 2012, p. 83)

Over half a billion dollars in penalties and no changes were made in the leadership of Goldman Sachs in the wake of the settlement with the SEC. Goldman Sachs settled a civil lawsuit before it went through an incredibly long trial and appeals process for more than half a billion dollars. According to the press release posted by the Huffington Post on 15 July 2010, and then updated again 25 May 2011, Goldman Sachs made the following admission in federal court documents:

> Goldman acknowledges that the marketing materials for the ABACUS 2007-AC1 transaction contained incomplete information. In particular, it was a mistake for the Goldman marketing materials to state that the reference portfolio was "selected by" ACA

> Management LLC without disclosing the role of
> Paulson & Co. Inc. in the portfolio selection process
> and that Paulson's economic interests were adverse to
> CDO investors. Goldman regrets that the marketing
> materials did not contain that disclosure. (para 6)

The upshot of the settlement however was that the trouble with
the SEC was over and Goldman was able to get back down to
business. Further, the settlement actually increased Goldman's
market cap resulting a nearly 10% rise in stock value
immediately following the announcement. Goldman still made
massive profits despite the record setting profits, and other than
changes in how bonuses are paid out, there has not been any
substantial change in Goldman's operations or personnel.
(Jennings, 2012, p. 81-82 and Huffington Post, 2011, paras. 7-
12)

While it is clear that there were significant monetary damages,
some of which were addressed in the SEC's civil suit, the real
damage is the impact of ABACUS and from similar deals made
by other banks in the same manner. We might argue that as a
society, everyone wants a home, despite the fact that not
everyone can afford it, or at least in some cases, many struggle
to manage their finances so that they can afford it. In the end,
as Professor William Black from the University of Missouri-
Kansas City has suggested, the ultimate victims of the collapse
of the CDO market are the US Government, the US taxpayers,
and the folks who bought homes that should never have done
so in the first place.

The concern that the Goldman Sachs case creates is that it calls
into question the efficacy of our system of enforcement

regarding the protections provided to investors and consumers under the law.   If the über-wealthy, be they individuals or corporations, are able to fleece sophisticated investors, and still walk away relatively unscathed is that okay?   Considering the damage that was caused, it seems that there was insufficient impact on Goldman Sachs to deter it from continuing to operate as it has since the early 20th Century, nor for that matter, enough force in the penalty to create a deterrent to prevent others from doing the same thing.   The failure of the SEC to ensure that all investors recouped their losses when Goldman Sachs has the financial ability to do so is weak at best, and at worst lacking the ring of ethical fairness and moral authority.

8.0   Conclusion

There is a variety of ethical systems available for the businessperson to work with. The fact that there is no universal consensus on how these should be viewed, understood and applied suggests that there will continue to be moral and ethical failures in business. It is a shortsighted fallacy to believe that regulation is the panacea for the ethical failures that periodically strike the economy.   The human ability to rationalize, the temporary satisfaction of greed, and the decisions people make to follow through on will continue to impact stakeholders be they customers, employees or investors.

Training an individual with the rationale for solid business ethic and providing additional motivation to follow through via enforcement of regulation provides reasonable extrinsic motivation. Nevertheless, if the shaping of extrinsic, external motivations for ethical decision-making does not translate to an intrinsic sense of value, all ethical systems will fail. It is the ability of the human mind and heart to justify and rationalize that weakens the impact that a good business school can have. The building of character into the individual begins before they ever enter the workforce. Thus, ethical failures are first and foremost a failure in the moral character of the individual. If the foundation is cracked (i.e. moral character) then the structure will probably fail (i.e. ethical character). In the end, penalties ought to be applied to present an impediment to further ethics violations, but they will never prevent them from happening.

How does this apply in the Goldman Sachs' case? It begs the question that was originally posed, were the penalties imposed upon Goldman Sachs' sufficient? If the spirit of the law, but not the letter of the law, is violated, is it then appropriate to penalize a corporation for doing what it is supposed to do: compete on the open market and generate a profit as best it can?

Or, is it truly a case of Goldman Sachs being "too big to fail." The politicos would have us believe that the failures of multiple banks would have been more disastrous to the economy than allowing the market to correct itself. And yet, by subsidizing Goldman's failures which are now known to be self-created at least in part and also apparently admittedly by design, the Federal Government has largely undermined the efficacy of ethical enforcement. This leads to the final question that needs to be answered, are bailouts an appropriate response for a corporation that has effectively, if not legally, defrauded clients, or investors, to the tune of billions of dollars? Perhaps some corporations are large enough that catastrophic failure could make the nation's economic woes worse. However, the latest episode of ethics failures has been partly to blame for the world economy struggling. Perhaps, a reasonable solution to an ethical dilemma that lacks the clearly defined lines of black & white might follow these lines:

1. Corporations that commit serious ethics violations cannot maintain leadership in the face of a bailout.
2. If the government is bailing an organization out, then leadership may be required to change.
3. If the government is bailing an organization out, then a plan needs to be drawn by industry experts and implemented to ensure that the failure is not repeated.
4. If the government is bailing an organization out, and it is shown that clients or investors lost money as a result of ethics violations on the part of employees or executives of that firm, then no deal can be struck to settle without ensuring that 100% of the losses sustained are repaid.

What makes the Goldman Sachs' settlement particularly troublesome is that going all the way back to the Internet/Dot.Com failures of the late 1990s, there has been no effort by Goldman Sachs to make its clients' losses whole again. While the balance of the world's economic woes cannot be placed solely on the shoulders of Goldman Sachs, they should have been held to a higher standard in the direct case of their clients' egregious losses.

9.0   References

---. (2012, January 12). Economic Crisis and Market Upheaval. *The New York Times.* Retrieved 12 January 2012, from http://topics.nytimes.com/top/reference/timestopics/subjects/c/credit_crisis/index.html?offset=0&s=newest.

Jennings, Marianne M (2012). *Business ethics: Case studies and selected readings* 7th Ed. Mason, OH: South-Western Cengage Learning.

Huffington Post. (2011, May 25). Goldman Sachs SEC SETTLEMENT Reached -- And Stock SOARS. *HuffingtonPost.Com.* Retrieved 8 January 2012, from http://www.huffingtonpost.com/2010/07/15/goldman-sachs-sec-settlem_n_648045.html

moral. 2012. In *Merriam-Webster.com.* Retrieved January 12, 2012, from http://www.merriam-webster.com/dictionary/moral.

BONUS #3:
Rick Santorum is Right
about Family & Economic Growth

ABSTRACT – *doctoral research essay*

The modern American business corporation finds its roots in the development of the religious and political development of the American Colonies, with indirect ties to the British use of the corporation to aid in economic growth and providing for bequests to churches. The rapid and extensive growth of corporations in early America directly contributed to the rapid economic growth that far outpaced that of Britain and Europe at the same time. Understanding the role of stakeholder influence on the operations of the corporation is timely and important as it directly relates to our political freedom and our ability to determine our own economic future. The failure to understand this may lead to a loss of self-governance and the loss of economic freedom if social democracy is allowed to progress unrestrained. Finally, blaming the corporation for the ills that plague society is both ill-advised and ignorant of the truth. The corporation is not a conscienceless organization that seeks profit to the detriment of all else, but is the organizational form that provides for political, economic and religious organization, coordination and growth. Finally, the failure to recognize the role of the nuclear family, in relation to the corporation as an engine for economic growth and political self-determination is poorly understood.

Table of Contents

Santorum is Right: Capitalism and the Corporation

1.0   Introduction

The corporation as a concept has been present for centuries, but the modern business corporation in the American sense has only existed since Colonial times (Jennings, 2012, pp. 105 – 106). The question to be examined is whether or not there are clearly discernible dangers poised to strike at the modern American business corporation. Michael Novak writes "The business corporation is once again in a fight for is life, and the sooner the dangers than [*sic*] menace it are exactly discerned the better" (Jennings, 2012, p. 108).

2.0   How long has the corporation existed?

Michael Novak relates in his article on Capitalism and the corporation relates that the corporation began in Medieval Europe with the creation of burial societies (Jennings, 2012, p. 106). Avner Greif (2006) relates in more detail a discussion regarding the origin of the modern corporation as having roots in Medieval Europe:

Corporations are defined as consistent with their historical meaning: intentionally created, voluntary, interest-based, and self-governed permanent associations. Guilds, fraternities, universities, communes, and city-states are some of the corporations that have historically dominated Europe; businesses and professional associations, business corporations, universities, consumer groups, counties, republics, and democracies are examples of corporations in modern societies …. European economic growth in the late medieval period was based on an unprecedented institutional complex of corporations and nuclear families, which, interestingly, still characterizes the West. More generally, European history suggests that this complex was conducive to long-term growth, although we know little about why this was the case or why it is difficult to transplant this complex to other societies. (p. 308)

In light of the foregoing, it is reasonable to suggest that the modern concept of the corporation finds its roots in Western Civilization between 1000 and 1,200 years ago. Second, it has been specifically tied to the growth of both self-governance and rapid economic growth.

3.0   Compare & Contrast USA Corporations with European Corporations

The importance of the rise of the corporation in Western Civilization cannot be understated. The rise of freedom and self-governance has been directly attributed to the development of the corporation. Avner Greif (2006) writes:

... successful corporations fostered the beliefs and norms that justify and support self-governance, the rule of law, the legitimacy of majority rule, respect for minority rights, individualism, and trust among non-kin. Indeed, cross-country regressions indicate that a country's growth and the stability of its democracy increase the longer its historical democratic experience has been (Torsten Persson and Guido Tabellini, 2005). (p. 311)

In other words, it is the corporation and those traits it encourages are part and parcel of how the freedom of the self-governed developed.

While the roots of the American business corporation are clearly rooted specifically in the development of the British corporation, the differences between the two were clear from earliest colonial times and diverged further from then on. While England did begin to develop corporations rapidly initially around the time of the early colonization efforts in

220 | P a g e   Rules & Religion: *Wrecking America*

North America, it was the passage of the Bubble Act in 1720 that severely restricted the formation of corporations in the United Kingdom (Seavoy, 1978, pp. 31-32). Novak indicates that the American business corporation developed separately from that of the British corporation to the "shock of royal prerogative on the other side of the Atlantic" (Jennings, 2012, p. 106). The intent of meaning being that the granting of corporate powers in the United Kingdom was more about privilege granted by the Crown, and less about the recognition of a public service provided by the proposed corporation as was the custom in the Colonies. Colonial corporations were formed with significant regularity and in large numbers, such that their formation was neither constrained by British Common Law, nor particularly informed by it as well. (Jennings, 2012, p. 106 & Seavoy, 1978, pp. 30-33)

Novak suggests that the critical difference between the American corporation and the British corporation is that in America the state essentially retained only the right to approve and register applications for corporate charter and was not responsible for granting them, as was the case in Britain (Jennings, 2012, p. 106). Writes Novak:

The corporation, to survive, could no longer depend on its privileges; it could survive only if it met the needs of its customers and the purposes of its investors. It brought civil society not only independence from the state but also unparalleled social flexibility and a zest for risk and dare. (Jennings, 2012, p. 106)

An additional difference not noted by Novak (Jennings, 2012), but reviewed by Seavoy (1978), was the importance of the general incorporation replacing the cumbersome English system of trusts for ecclesiastical organizations (pp. 39 – 40).

The upshot of which was a radical shift away from state sponsored religion, and a furtherance of the American ideal of religious freedom. In summation, the differences between the American corporation and the British corporation are who, meaning the political authority, issued the charter granting permission to incorporate, the purposes allowable thereto, and the somewhat removed issue of religion.

4.0   **What are the two definitions of stakeholders according to Novak?**

Michael Novak provides two distinct definitions of stakeholder and relates one as it follows in the development and application of the Homestead Act and as well one in the social democratic sense (Jennings, 2012, p. 107):

In this context, *stakeholder* means *owner* and private *risk taker*. The purpose of an arrangement of society into many private stakeholders is to secure the *general* welfare and the larger *public* interest. The stakeholder society in this sense is the very foundation of the free society … The social democratic sense of the term *stakeholder* is quite different. Stakeholders are all those who deem themselves entitled to make demands on the system and to receive from it. (Jennings, 2012, p. 107)

Novak has expanded the discussion regarding stakeholders in the organizational sense to a broader societal meaning wherein the question of national governance is impacted by an understanding of how *stakeholder* is defined. Benjamin Neville and Bulent Menguc (2006) developed an excellent piece regarding the interactions of multiple stakeholders within a system, and a nation is unquestionably also a system, though it is significantly more complex than a business corporation (p. 377).

Neville and Menguc (2006) write, "… stakeholders possessing power have the ability to exercise their own will despite resistance (Weber, 1947)" (p. 378). The American system is at war within itself as regards concepts of stakeholder theory in a political sense, as borne out in legislation (i.e. the welfare system, and now many highly contested attempts to reform that system). Framed in the context of Novak's definition, this can be more completely defined as a debate concerned whether America will continue to be a free society of stakeholders freely associating and organizing into groups, also known as corporations, or a society wherein stakeholders are entitled to make demands for individuals upon the system as a whole (Jennings, 2012, p. 107). Novak's definitions are less concerned with their application to the individual corporation though the concept is implicit therein.

Ronald Seavoy (1978) provides a cogent description of the development of the corporation in America and specifically examines the states of New York and Massachusetts to elucidate his points (pp. 33 – 60). While not explicitly linear, Seavoy (1978) attributes the rapid economic growth in New York State to as being prefaced by the need to create corporations for religious and educational purposes, with the most notable being teaching reading as a skill as it related to the necessary spiritual undertaking of reading and understanding the Bible (pp. 33 – 60). This became the basis for the rapid expansion of the formation and use of the corporation economically, as there was already an established understanding of how to form corporations. Seavoy (1978) writes:

The religious and secular desire to achieve mass literacy in New York had produced a considerable number of men in each community experienced in organizing corporations, and the experience gained in organizing benevolent corporations appears to have been a major local training ground for adaptive entrepreneurs ... The organizers who successfully institutionalized the transfer of New England's religious and educational goals to New York appear to have, in the process, trained a disproportionately large number of men who had the confidence to use the organizing skills to promote and manage newer types of public service enterprises, many of which were profit-seeking. (Seavoy, 1978, p. 60)

This development in America is important to stakeholder definition and theory as it is directly attributable as a foundational concept in the socio-economic development of the nation. The application synthesizes well with Novak (Jennings, 2012) who writes that this is important because "Americans believed ... that the common good is better serve by a regime of private property than by common ownership or state ownership" (p. 107). In other words, freedom and self-governance are driven through the concepts of private property and the ownership thereof.

Neville and Menguc (2006) write about the mediating effects of multiple stakeholders of a corporation, which places the emphasis on the corporate organization, and is less concerned with the Novak's (Jennings, 2012) definition that is more concerned with the political implications for self-governance. Neville and Menguc (2006) are specifically concerned with describing the effects that multiple stakeholders have upon the individual corporation and provide the macro-categories of stakeholders as being government, customers and employees (pp. 382 – 384).

Stakeholder definition and theory are important to the individual corporation as it is important to be able to identify and then work with the critical influences that impact the corporation's ability to function, grow and derive profit. In Novak's (Jennings, 2012) definition of *stakeholder*, the definition is important to understand in terms of political governance and the succeeding impacts on the individual's ability and the corporation's ability (as an organized individual entity) to self-govern, derive profit, and contribute to the overall growth and development of the nation.

5.0   The Effects of Social Democracy & Danger of Perpetual Demand

Summing up Novak's (Jennings, 2012) definition of the stakeholder under social democratic theory could be the tyranny of the many foisted on the few, or desires of the many forced upon the individual (p. 107). Novak (Jennings, 2012) writes:

… a "stakeholder society" is one in which each citizen is entitled to make claims on others according to his or her needs. These needs are infinitely expansive, however, so perpetual dissatisfaction is guaranteed … our longings are infinite, beyond all earthly satisfaction … Its schemes of social belonging usually end up with populations far too accustomed to receiving and demanding. Those most skilled at mobilizing demands fare best. (p. 107)

The stakeholder society, or social democratic definition of stakeholder, results in runaway need as there is no balancing influence for personal responsibility (Jennings, 2012, p. 107).

Jerry Muller (2007) provides support to Novak's (Jennings, 2012) assertions regarding the threats of a social democratic society, though he expresses it differently. In his examination, Muller (2007) examines the writings of Adam Smith, Edmund Burke, John Stuart Mill, Vilfredo Pareto, Friedrich Hayek and many others (pp. 77 – 86). Hayek quoted by Muller (2007) echoes the sentiments of Alexis de Tocquevile quoted by Novak (Jennings, 2012), when he writes:

After a lifetime of reflecting upon the hazards posed by democracy to capitalism and to liberalism, Hayek asked rhetorically, "Is there really no other way for people to maintain a democratic government than by handing over unlimited power to a group of elected representatives whose decisions must be guided by the exigencies of a bargaining process in which they bribe a sufficient number of voters to support an organized group of themselves numerous enough to outvote the rest?" (p. 86)

Which while it should be a scathing reprimand for the failure of those in elected office who fail to serve the greater good, Muller (2007) does suggest the following issues as being a threat to capitalism under a democracy: "… difficulties created by economic ignorance on the part of politicians and voters, the influence of the irrational forces of envy and guilt, and the rational but self-defeating forces leading to inflation" (p. 86). The end result of each of the quoted challenges that face capitalism in democracy, which if left unaddressed, or unmanaged, result either in the destruction of the corporation due to the failure to generate a profit, or in the loss of the freedoms most would choose to enjoy. As a result, it is not inappropriate to say that if any man wishes to be free then he must fight the irrational forces of social democracy as they lead to the tyranny of many over the interests of the few thus making society as whole, all the poorer. If allowed to run amuck, it can even lead to the disintegration of a society's ability to sustain itself.

6.0   The corporation is "not a cold meteor fallen from the sky"

Lowenstein (2011) writing about The Occupy Wall Street for Bloomberg movement details a vocal effort that is precisely echoing what Edmund Burke complained about almost two centuries ago: "The poor, Burke complained, envied and resented the rich without understanding the function of the rich in accumulating capital, and so were apt to act against their own interests" (Muller, 2007, p. 80).   While it may be politically expedient to decry profiteering and massive compensation on the part of mega multinational corporations, it is not economically wise or intellectually accurate.

Novak's (Jennings, 2012) statement that "the corporation is not a cold meteor fallen from the skies" provides a poetic and powerful image regarding what the corporation is (p. 108). The origin of the corporation is in the roots of religious and economic freedom and directly tied to the education of the population. The contributions of the corporation to society are important because with very few exceptions, most organizations of people from local government, to the churches in our communities, to the large multinational corporations that create jobs are all corporations.

The failures of individuals within corporations, and the failures of individual corporations to provide a public good do not eliminate the overall benefit the corporation provides in the self-organization of a civil society.

Making an enemy of the corporation and its necessary drive to produce wealth belies not only its importance to society, but also the mediating factor it has in guaranteeing our political freedoms and our economic self-determination. What Novak (Jennings, 2012) is saying is that to make an enemy of the corporation, and the internal failures it struggles with, is essentially a schizophrenic argument about our economic system, as well as our system of government. While Novak (Jennings, 2012), admits that there are challenges that need to addressed, he is absolutely correct in calling for a sane, coherent and fully informed understanding as to the role and benefit of the corporation in securing our freedoms and partnering in our prosperity. (Jennings, 2012, p. 106 – 108)

7.0   Conclusion

It is important to note that the dangers facing the corporation are both internal and external. The internal dangers that threaten the modern business corporations continued utility and existence are at least in part due to a failure to manage its relationships with internal stakeholders (employees) and its communication with external stakeholders, namely customers and government (Neville and Menguc, 2006, pp. 380 – 382). The external dangers to the modern business corporation include monetary and fiscal policy (inflation and stagflation), political pressures created by ignorant politicians and voters (moves toward increased social democracy), as well as poorly managing competition in the global marketplace. (Jennings, 2012, p. 108 and, Muller, 2007, pp. 80 – 86)

However, the chief challenge to our economic and political freedoms is the failure to understand the connection between the corporation and the nuclear family. (Goss, 2010 and Greif, 2006) Goss (2010) asserts that the current failures in corporate ethics are directly related to a failure of the nuclear family, and references the assertion by historians that the disintegration of the family contributed to the fall of the Roman Empire (p. 49 –

52).   However, it is Grief (2006) that succinctly relates the importance of the family and our failure thus far to understand the connection between the family and economic growth (p. 311). He writes:

Whatever the implications of corporation-based institutions may be, the relationship between their emergence and the nuclear family structure suggests that we have more to learn regarding   distinct   institutional—and,   hence,   growth— trajectories and their persistence by examining the dynamic interplay   between   family   structures   and   institutional development. (p. 311)

8.0 References

Fitchett, J. A. (2005). Consumers as stakeholders: prospects for democracy in marketing theory. *Business Ethics: A European Review, 14*(1), 14-27. doi:10.1111/j.1467-8608.2005.00383.x

Goss, B. (2010) Rules & Religion: Wrecking America. *Unpublished manuscript.*

Greif, A. (2006). Family Structure, Institutions, and Growth: The Origins and Implications of Western Corporations. *American Economic Review, 96*(2), 308-312.

Jennings, Marianne M (2012). *Business ethics: Case studies and selected readings* 7th Ed. Mason, OH: South-Western Cengage Learning.

Leap, T., & Loughry, M. L. (2004). The stakeholder-friendly firm. *Business Horizons, 47*(2), 27. doi:10.1016/j.bushor.2003.07.002

Lowenstein, R. (2011). IT'S NOT A HIPPIE THING. (cover story). *Bloomberg BusinessWeek,* (4252), 69-72.

Mitchell, L. E. (2006). The relevance of corporate theory to corporate and economic development: Comment on the transplantation of the legal discourse on corporate personality theories. *Washington and Lee Law Review, 63*(4), 1489-1502. Retrieved from http://search.proquest.com/docview/236271850?accountid=28180

moral. (2011). Merriam-Webster.com. *Merriam Webster Dictionary.* Merriam-Webster, Inc. Retrieved 8 January 2012. Retrieved from http://www.merriam-webster.com/dictionary/moral.

Muller, J. Z. (2007). The democratic threat to capitalism. *Daedalus, 136*(3), 77-86. Retrieved from http://search.proquest.com/docview/210574434?accountid=28180

Neville, B. A., & Menguc, B. (2006). Stakeholder multiplicity: Toward an understanding of the interactions between stakeholders. *Journal of Business Ethics, 66*(4), 377-391. doi:10.1007/s10551-006-0015-4

Seavoy, R. E. (1978). The public service origins of the American business corporation. *Business History Review (Pre-1986), 52*(000001), 30-30. Retrieved from http://search.proquest.com/docview/205456846?accountid=28180

BONUS #4:
Proposing an Ethical Construct for Business

ABSTRACT (Expansion of thoughts introduced in Chapter 12)

What is meant by the term "business ethics?" Is the term appropriate, or an utter misnomer? Most Americans are familiar with the bloated failures in the practice of ethics on the part of such large entities as WorldCom, Anderson Consulting, and Enron. The author provides an examination of articles written by four notable authorities in business management: Alahmad, Drucker, Friedman and Murphy. The author asserts that there is excellent support to the definition of and greater understanding for a personal ethical decision making process. However, the author remains unconvinced that this should also translate to a comprehensive effort to define a business ethic. The author proposes the development of a three dimensional ethical construct (3DEC) to aid in helping individuals understand their ethical decision making process and then linking it to known ethical theories. The information gathered, and the comprehension gained, can be a starting point for increased understanding across national boundaries or cultural divides. However, it can also become the post upon which we pillory the failures of an individual for failing to meet an unexpressed cultural norm. In the end, the process of quantifying a personal ethic or business ethic is dangerously subjective.

Table of Contents

Proposing an Ethical Construct for Business Ethics

1.0   Introduction

The businessmen [that] believe that they are defending free enterprise when they declaim that business is not concerned "merely" with profit but also with promoting desirable "social" ends … are … preaching pure and unadulterated socialism. Businessmen who talk this way are unwitting puppets of the intellectual forces that have been undermining the basis of free society these past decades. (Friedman, 1970, para. 1)

What is meant by the term "business ethics?" Is the term appropriate, or an utter misnomer? Most Americans are familiar with the bloated failures in the practice of ethics on the part of such large entities as WorldCom, Anderson Consulting, and Enron. As these incredible failures have rippled effects across the business and financial landscape as well as the emotional psyche of the country, articles have been written decrying the failure of these large corporations to practice sound business ethics. There are calls for the business schools to teach something more than simply how best to generate profits. Peter Drucker (1981) writes

There are countless seminars on it, speeches, articles, conferences and books, not to mention the many earnest attempts to write "business ethics" into the law …. Ethics is, after all, not a recent discovery. Over the centuries, philosophers in their struggle with human behavior have developed different approaches to ethics …. (p. 18).

Milton Friedman (1970) writing for the New York Times Magazine, penned the following: "The first step toward clarity in examining the doctrine of social responsibility of business is to ask precisely what it implies for whom" (para 2). An articulate conversation that is both meaningful and useful cannot occur unless an understanding of not only what business ethics are, but also to whom they are applicable. Ala' Alahmad (2010) suggests that "one of the main problems that we face in the world today is the lack of ethical leadership" (p. 31). But, if there is a lack of coherence in the discussion as multiple researchers and authors suggest, then is the problem solvable?

Society is capable of solving the problem of ethical failures. However, the answers do not lie with the abilities of individuals nor do they lie with capabilities of either government or businesses. The answers lie within the depths of the mind of the individual, but not in an unspecific, insubstantial self-help, think positive manner. Rather it is critical to understand that, both as individuals and as a society, the power of belief is the basis on which all ethics, business or otherwise, flow. Many discussions regarding ethics focus on the manner of how decisions are made. While no exhaustive research regarding ethics research or discussions have been conducted for this effort, the ad hoc finding is that most approaches do not typically seek to understand or confront underlying assumptions. These assumptions comprise the filter, or matrix, that an individual uses in determining solutions for ethical dilemmas. In other words:

- Beliefs precede our thoughts.
- Thoughts precede actions and words.
- The consequences of words and actions impact beliefs only if those beliefs are not strongly held.
- If beliefs are strongly held, the closer they relate to an individual's personal identity. As a result, no matter the consequences, the less likely it is that those beliefs will change. (Goss, 2010, p. 49).

The contrast between a personal ethic and a business ethic should not be vastly different. The ability to make an ethically sound decision can be demonstrated in a variety of ways. For example, for some as they relate to the practice of religious beliefs the ethic of a universal and objective standard is clear. For others, one finds a sliding scale of moral relativism in the expression and application of political beliefs. The philosophy of governance, whether it is for business, for politics or for the practice of religion is ultimately shaped by the beliefs within the individual. However, rather than calling it religion, it should be called what it actually is: a belief system.

While there are some who claim to have no religious faith or belief system, they have failed to recognize that this is in and of itself a belief structure. Perhaps a broader and more appropriate definition of religion is that faith, or belief, is what structures and drives a world view. Therefore, the author respectfully submits for the readers' consideration that any discussion of ethics is incomplete without the concept of an integrated world view. This means that ethics, the morals and norms of a person's belief system, are actively integrated with the individual's words, actions and attitudes.

A responsible approach to business ethics should recognize that people do not typically make decisions in a formulaic, defined manner that proceeds to interpret options through the filter of a defined ethic. In an effort to further refine the attempt to measure business ethics conducted by Reidenbach and Robin, Randall Hansen (1992) asked the following in his introduction: "How does a manager know how to make decisions when faced with ethical dilemmas? Would the manager make a 'gut' decision, seek advice from peers, use a rule of thumb, or some combination of all three?" (p. 523). The stated purpose of the research conducted by Reidenbach and Robin (1988, 1990) and Hansen (1992) was "to develop a scale

… that could distinguish the processes individuals use in evaluating ethical situations and choosing solutions" (Hansen, 1992, p. 533). Unfortunately, while a complex scale has been somewhat developed, there is no clear, practical and therefore useful scale as a result. Understanding the process of how individuals make ethical decisions has not provided a corresponding conclusion providing an application for the results.

That "Business Ethics" is an artificially narrow and therefore less than useful concept is put forward by Friedman (1970) when he writes:

The discussions of the "social responsibilities of business" are notable for their analytical looseness and lack of rigor. What does it mean to say that "business" has responsibilities? Only people can have responsibilities. A corporation is an artificial person and in this sense may have artificial responsibilities, but "business" as a whole cannot be said to have responsibilities, even in this vague sense (para. 2)

This analysis is reinforced by the truth that while corporations may pay financial penalties for the actions of its officers, managers or employees, a corporation itself cannot be imprisoned. Rather it is the officers, managers or employees that commit the offense that are prosecuted.

Randall Hansen (1992) explains that there are at least 13 different models for defining the ethical constructs used by managers in business (p. 533). However, despite the wide variety of ethical models that currently exists, Hansen writes "Murphy and Laczniak (1981) have pointed out that almost all normative theories in moral philosophy can be classified as either deontological or teleological" (p. 532). In light of the forgoing, it is more appropriate to assert that ethics, business or otherwise, are really the individual expression of a personal moral philosophy, regardless of the setting.   Therefore, business ethics is a misnomer as the term "business" simply places the expression or exercise of an individual's morality in a specific context. The question that should be asked is: "What is the ethical construct from which an individual is operating?" The follow up question is, "Once we know the answer of what the construct, or ethical decision matrix, what does one do with the information?"

2.0   Academicians: Discussion of Business Ethics

Milton Friedman (2010) suggests that are two mechanisms that create the components that drive business and society, the market   mechanism   and   the   political   mechanism. Understanding how these components interact with society and shape the environment within which business operates is important. Regarding the market mechanism, he writes:

The   political   principle   that   underlies   the   market mechanism is unanimity... [that] there are no values, no 'social' responsibilities in any sense other than the shared values and responsibilities of individuals.   Society is a collection of individuals and of the various groups, they voluntarily form. (para. 30)

Regarding the political mechanism, he writes:

The   political   principle   that   underlies   the   political mechanism is conformity. The individual must serve a more general social interest – whether that is determined by a church, a dictator or a majority. The individual may have a vote and say in what is to be done, but if he is overruled, he must conform. (para. 31)

While Friedman agrees that the political mechanism cannot be avoided entirely, he suggests that "there is one and only one social responsibility of business – to use its resources and engage in activities designed to increase its profits so long as it stays within the rules of the game ..." (para. 33). He calls the concept of social responsibility for business "'a fundamentally subversive doctrine' in a free society" (para. 33).

Patrick Murphy (2010) suggests that it is comprehension and ability to act that comprise responsibility, that which is a premise that underlies sound ethics (p. 245). He writes,

At its most fundamental level, responsibility pertains to an entity's ability to respond to a person, situation, or issue in a certain way. Implicit in these words is that one must be able to consciously understand the scope of these responsibilities and be able to act on them. (p. 245)

However, while Murphy continues to discuss the manner in which responsibility and ethic can be understood in the context of seven different applications, and as well argues eloquently for understanding responsibility as a foundational aspect of Corporate Social Responsibility (CSR), he does not controvert his initial fundamental assessment: understanding and the ability to act. From previous research conducted with Enderle, Murphy suggests that there are three components to corporate responsibility:

A. Who is responsible
B. To Whom it is responsible
C. For what is the corporation responsible (p. 246)

However, even in the midst of defining what CSR is, or should comprise, one finds that the discussion still reverts to the importance of the individual. In fact, Murphy (2010) writes "These three categories focus on who in the organization bears ultimate responsibility for an action and on the fact that any decision impacts multiple stakeholders" (p. 246). Thus, while calling for CSR investment, understanding and study, there is still recognition of the importance of the individual(s) making decisions that impact stakeholders.

Peter Drucker (1981) is quite strident in a colorful decry of business ethics. He writes:

...only *law* can handle the rights and objections of collectives. *Ethics is always a matter of the person*....[*italics* Drucker, underline mine]

"Business ethics," this discussion should have made clear, is to ethics what soft porn is to the Platonic Eros; soft porn too talks of something it calls "love." And insofar as "business ethics" comes even close to ethics, it comes close to casuistry and will, predictably, end up as a fig leaf for the shameless and as special pleading for the powerful and the wealthy. (Drucker, 1981, p. 34)

But even while he denounces the concept of business ethics, Drucker (1981) still presents two ethical concepts: "the Ethics of Prudence" for "anonymous" and "highly visible" leaders and the "Ethics of Interdependence" an understanding of the interrelationships between organizations based upon a Confucian philosophy (p. 34 – 36). But, even the Ethics of Interdependence carry responsibilities for the individual to practice.

Ala' Alahmad (2010) calls for the development of an international code of ethics for leadership (p. 32). He acknowledges that an inculcate sense of right and wrong is not universal, though "there are two general views of ethics: relativist and universalist (Donaldson, 1994)" (Alahmad, 2010, p. 31). He admits that individuals choose their own ethical frame of reference and then asks if there is even a "universalistic" sense of ethics. "Ethics," he defines, "are a person's concept of right and wrong" (Alahmad, 2010, p. 31). In the end, Alahmad proposes a rule of thumb, or guideline, with basic definitions that anyone in a position of leadership worldwide should apply. This guide calls on every leader in any sphere whether political, educational or economic (business or corporate) to act "in most instances [with] – honesty, tell the truth no matter what, respect, punctuality, not judgmental, just, humble and dignity" (Alahmad, 2010, p. 34). While his research indicates that opinions are greatly varied on the practicality and existence of a universal ethic, the entire approach might be reduced to just one primary ingredient: dignity. Perhaps by acknowledging the humanity and therefore granting dignity to any human being for their humanity will enable the leader to operate in reasonable expression of each aspect of Alahmad's proposed code of ethics.

Of four business management authorities examined herein, Alahmad, Friedman, Drucker and Murphy, Ala' Alahmad is the most generic and least useful. Friedman (1981) is nearly entirely focused on the importance of a personal ethic, and that CSR is subversive to the aims of a free society. Drucker (1981) emphasizes the personal ethic in his "Ethics of Prudence, but allows for a corporate (business) ethic in his description of an "Ethics of Interdependence." Murphy (2010) calls for a well-defined sense of CSR for the corporation, which he suggests is beyond the responsibility of the individual's ethic. Alahmad (2010) acknowledges that a global, or universal, concept of ethics for leaders internationally does not exist, believes it needs to be developed (p. 34).

None of the authors provide a practical manner in which to engage in the discussion of ethics, nor do they suggest a tool that would be useful to an employee, a manager, or an executive in gaining a useful picture of the practice of ethical decision making. If one were to place the four authors on a continuum from emphasizing a personal ethic versus the expression of a corporate ethic, the author proposes the following graphic (see figure 2.1). Throughout all four authors, there is a strong emphasis on the importance of a personal ethic even while two suggest a corporate level of responsibility.

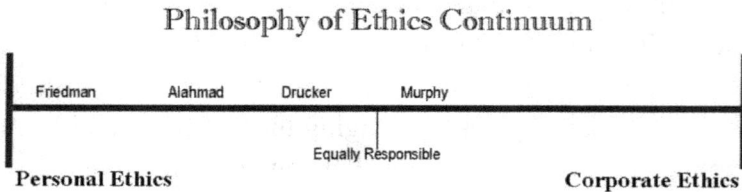

Philosophy of Ethics Continuum

Friedman	Alahmad	Drucker	Murphy

Equally Responsible

Personal Ethics   **Corporate Ethics**

Murphy (2010) calls for CSR, whereas Drucker (1981) allows for it, though somewhat de-emphasized to the expression of an individual leader's expression of the "Ethics of Prudence." Alahmad (2010) never addresses the concept of CSR, and Friedman (1981) outright denounces the concept of CSR.

3.0   Proposing an Ethical Construct

Randall Hansen (1992) concluded that existing research demonstrates

… that individuals use four evaluation dimensions when making decisions with ethical implications: a broad-based ethical judgment evaluation, a deontological judgment evaluation, a teleological judgment evaluation, and a social contract evaluation. (p. 533)

However, there is no real effort that enables the description of the ethical decision making process to be understood in a manner that provides an easily understandable application of the information, once the process has been defined. If a manager, executive, or employee understands that a certain ethic is the predominant process for whomever, what does one do with that information? Are we, as a society, going to begin regulating the ethical decision making process of others? In a faint echo of Friedman, the author suggests that to attempt to regulate thoughts and opinions is neither wise, nor practical.

Mark Schwartz and James Weber (2006) proposed the further development of the "Business Ethics National Index (BENI)" in a jointly researched and presented article for *Business and Society*, in the September 2006 issue. Their idea was to develop a tool that could be used not only to further research into ethics around the globe, but hopefully to also create a web-based database of information relating to ethics internationally (p. 402). The creation of the BENI as a tool holds "three primary purposes":

(a) help guide the direction of future descriptive business ethics research

(b) allow for a more robust descriptive and normative evaluation of cross-national comparisons of business ethics activity, and

(c) provide an additional means by which to encourage additional formal business ethics activities in a given country (Schwartz & Weber, 2006, p. 383).

Further, the BENI describes seven dimensions that ought to be measured on a national basis:

(a) academia
(b) business
(c) social or ethical investment
(d) business ethics organizations

(e) government activity

(f) social activist groups, and

(g) media coverage (Schwartz & Weber, 2006, p. 382)

The existence of several international indexes, "Transparency International's (2005) Corruption Perceptions Index," "the Civil Society Index (CSI) developed by CIVICUS (2004)," and "Account-Ability's National Corporate Responsibility Index (NCRI)" briefly described by Schwartz and Weber (2006), indicate that there is a movement to attempt to quantify and measure overall ethical environment for business internationally (p. 383). In their conclusion, the authors admit that having a BENI be useful on an international basis is difficult because "one must still struggle to locate empirical data allowing for accurate cross-country comparisons of national business ethics activity" (Schwartz & Weber, 2006, p. 402). Thus, the question of utility for any such index remains. What is the purpose for this measurement?

If it is as simple as the encouragement of nations that are traditionally known to struggle with graft, corruption and unfair business practices to seek to foster an environment that is safer for international business investment, then the purpose is not only admirable but also hopefully positive to fostering future global economic growth. However, if the efforts are intended to persuade and influence the actions of governments and their citizens along social and ethical investment, government action, social activist groups, and media coverage then the effort will most likely never achieve any kind of universal application. Countries that are known to struggle in the areas of trust will also struggle to accept the mores and norms of another society and may also see the effort as an attempt to unduly influence their country's sovereign self-governance. This point can be indirectly correlated from Alahmad's description of United Nations (UN) efforts in the development of its "Ethics Office and the Peace and Governance Programme" (p. 32 – 34). Their efforts have been described as "not capable of developing a code of ethics for international leaders" (Alahmad, 2010, p. 34).

If the efforts to measure and define a personal ethical model is difficult and complex, and the effort to measure at the national level is equally suspect, is there any reason to propose the development of an ethical construct? Yes. Provided that the following is true:

A. Limited to a personal ethic

B. Not specifically applied strictly to the corporate (business) level of activity

C. Universally applicable to anyone in any culture

D. Simple to understand, easy to apply in either a business or personal context

E. Useful if it helps the one taking the test understand their world view, *as they practice it, not how they believe it to be*

Socrates is known for having said that "the unexamined life is not worth living" (Kemmerling, 2001, para.11). In the same way, an ethical decision making model, or more simply put, the manner in which we make difficult decisions needs to be understood by the individual. Thus, the effort to help someone understand his or her own ethical construct is useful and important. In this manner, the perspective of the author is most closely aligned with that of Friedman (1981).

While the author agrees with the assertion of Randall Hansen, that the manner in which individuals solve ethical dilemmas is multi-dimensional, there is disagreement on the description of those dimensions (p. 533). Hansen (1992) writes that "individuals do not recognize the complete set of alternatives, and ... [that] Hunt and Vitell (1986) ... do not speculate on the reasons [why] ..." (p. 532). The author suggests that the reason for this is that the ethical decision making process is simpler than that originally described by Reidenbach & Robin and further refined by Hansen (1992, p. 523).

Therefore, the author proposes a three-dimensional ethical construct (3DEC). The concept behind the three dimensional model is to allow for a graphical representation of not only how individuals process ethical decisions, but also how they perceive the forces, internal and external that impact their decision making. Further, the author proposes that the development of a tool that provides for this measurement would have multiple applications in society today.

Figure 3.1 - Proposed 3D Ethical Construct (3DEC)

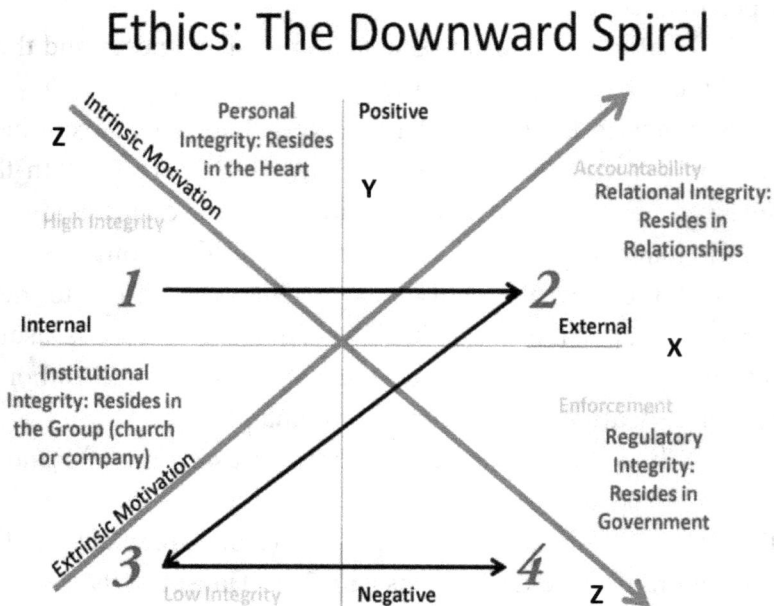

Ethics: The Downward Spiral

The proposed model is from an unpublished manuscript of the author (Goss, 2011, p. 49).

X. The scale along this plane (axis) is defined as a scale that describes where forces impact the individual as they make a choice described moving from Internal to External.

Y. The scale along this plane (axis) is defined as being the kind of force that is applied, moving from Negative to Positive flowing from the bottom of the model to the top. The connotation of negative versus positive relates to the nature of the forces typically present in the relationships providing the measure of influence.

Z. The scale along this plane (axis) moves from being defined high intrinsic-low extrinsic motivation in Quadrant One to low intrinsic – high extrinsic motivation in Quadrant Four. Intrinsic motivation means that motivation for quality ethical decisions are already within the person making the decision. Extrinsic motivation means that there is nothing necessarily within the person structuring decisions and ethics, rather it is being forced in some regulatory manner, whether through laws or group expectations. (Goss, 2011, p. 50)

Each of the axes, or planes as it is a 3D model, can then be tested for and produce results that can be graphically displayed in a manner similar to that of the DiSC® profile (2010). (Goss, 2011, pp. 49-50)

While it would be difficult to display the results as a true 3D construct, the effort to do it is reflective of the true nature of the individual, that of being a whole person. In other words, a holistic approach that attempts to elucidate the variety of forces that define the individual's ethical solution process is the only manner in which a true understanding can be drawn. Each section of the ethical construct has both a negative and a positive side to it, for a total of 8 distinct areas within the model. Though for simplicity, it will be easier to understand the model as having four primary quadrants. (Goss, 2010, pp. 49-50)

Quadrant one is defined as ***Character***. This is defined as being an area in which personal integrity is the primary driver for making ethic decisions. Some would refer to this as being heart-based, intrinsic motivation to make an excellent or highly ethical decision. This is defined as a positive area of influence because the power and influence for the decision comes from within the person. Consequences for violating an ethical value in this arena may not be very costly in terms of money, but they are likely to be costly in terms of self-perception. Self-perception includes both a sense of personal worth as well as a general sense of identity.

Quadrant two is defined as ***Accountability***. This is defined as being an area in which personal integrity is impacted, or based on the influence of the most influential relationships in an individual's life. This is any relationship that provides an external or more extrinsic basis for decision making. This is also defined as a positive area of influence. Consequences for violating an ethical value may cost someone a relationship, but may not result in the loss of vocation or income.

Quadrant three is defined as **Institutional** or **Corporate**. While one might argue that a corporate, or business environment is external to the individual, and it is, it is also still inside a group. The word corporate does not solely mean a business environment it can also refer to a religious group, a civic group, government organization and so on. Thus, internal in this context, refers to the fact that it is forces from within the group that create the impetus for decision. It is on the negative side of the Y axis, because it is group conformity that drives the decision. Thus, the force is intrinsic to the values of the group, but may or may not be intrinsic to the individual. The consequences for the violation of an ethical value may, at a minimum, cost someone economically in terms of position, income, and possibly relationships personal and professional.

Quadrant four is defined as ***Enforcement***. This is an area that is purely external to the individual and any group of which they may be a part. This is the lowest place on the ethical slide because it represents the least powerful impact on a person's decision making, though the consequences for violating ethics in this quadrant can be most severe including loss of income, loss of status, loss of position, and even a loss of freedoms previously enjoyed.

While the definition of these four quadrants is by no means exhaustive, it does seek to present a practical way in which to understand how individuals make ethical decisions. The hypothesis is that it will be universally applicable because it demonstrates the forces and the power that they exert on the individual without regard for their religious, cultural, economic, or political biases.

The ultimate aim for a three-dimensional ethical construct is the ability to create a visual graphic that would be useful in any context to help individuals understand either their own decision making process, or that of someone else's.

3.1.0 Proposed Test Design

In order to develop a reasonably consistent model for testing, the author suggests that a survey be developed with the following components:

- A bipolar seven-point Likert-itemized scale.

- Development of 10 scenario-based statements that relate to each section of the three-dimensional ethical construct for a total of 80 questions.
- A total of 32 additional questions (four questions per section), that will serve as control questions to determine consistency.
- Suggested format is an electronic survey to ensure ease of data capture and simplify the calculation and analysis process.
- Models already exist for such testing such as those produced by DiSC® (2010).

4.0   Application of Construct to Previously Articulated Points of View

The proposed 3D Ethical Construct (3DEC), as presented makes an attempt to harmonize the efforts and writings of the previously examined authorities on management, as well as the research of Hansen, Schwartz & Weber as follows:

4.1.0   As regarding Friedman (1981) ...

The model acknowledges the individual nature of ethical decision making and does not suggest a process that subverts the ultimate aim of business, to produce of profit for its owners.

4.1.2   As regarding Drucker (1981) ...

The model allows for an examination of the individual of their ethical decision making, and would enable them to consider it in relation to the "Ethics of Prudence." The "Ethics of Interdependence" becomes irrelevant in light of the new model.

4.1.0   As regarding Murphy (2010) ...

Once the individual better understands the manner in which ethical decisions are being made, they can then intelligently make solid ethical based decisions by being able to better understand their impact both personally and corporately.

4.1.0   As regarding Alahmad (2010) ...

Alahmad (2010) wanted to create a basis for an international code of ethics for leadership (p. 34). A tool such as this becomes useful in that it can engender productive conversation regarding what is considered ethical or unethical in other countries and in other cultures. If two individuals were willing to share their 3DEC profile, then it could assist with a more complete basis to proceed with understanding.

4.1.0   As regarding Hansen (1992) ...

The author agrees with Hansen that decisions are made in a multi-dimensional process. However, the author contends that the scale and manner of determining that process is complex and not practical for use in the marketplace. Thus, harmonization comes with recognition of the types of forces that impact ethical decision making, but also seeks to answer the questions that Hansen introduces, but never adequately answers.

4.1.0   As regarding Schwartz & Weber (2006) ...

The author agrees that it is helpful to have a broader understanding of the variety of influences that impact ethical decision making in other nations and other cultures. However, the author disagrees in the usefulness of the BENI. Rather, the author proposes that ethics researchers utilize a tool such as the proposed 3DEC to create a cultural profile from a sampling of the country or culture to engender understanding as to the operating environment for that country or culture.

5.0   **Call for More Research**

There is no question that ethical research and further development of research design is needed as the world seeks to expand its knowledge of ethical decision making. Not a single researcher or author has suggested that the field is known, or that the concept is conquered. As long as companies continue to experience epic failures, there will be continual debate and discussion as to what needs to be done about it.

Hansen (1992) wrote that "further research needs to be conducted to improve the scale and the interpretation of the findings" (p. 533). A better understanding of how ethical decisions are made should enable us as a society to avoid what Friedman terms "the external forces that curb the market … not … social conscience … [but] it will be the iron fist of Government bureaucrats" (para. 29). Murphy (2010) writes that

… Scholars need to define and better clarify what is meant by this amorphous term – responsibility. Empirical researchers hopefully can take cues from those working in trust to better articulate, clarify and operationalize the types of responsibility discussed here. (p. 251)

Ahlamad (2010) writes that there is no international code of ethics for leadership, and as a result, there is a vacuum in defining and understanding cross-culturally what makes right and wrong business decisions (p. 31 – 34). Drucker (1981) wrote that

… This discussion of the major approaches to ethics and of their concerns surely also shows that ethics has as much to say to the individual in our society of organizations as they ever had to say to the individual in earlier societies. They are just as important and just as needed nowadays. And they surely require hard and serious work. (p. 35)

Schwartz & Weber (2006) write that "information on business ethics activities around the world is desired by both researchers and practitioners" (p. 402). More research is needed, and will no doubt continue to be performed. However, what is measured and why it is measured is of critical importance. The "how" of ethical decision making is meaningless without understanding the "why" of ethical decision making, therefore, helping individuals to understand their own ethical decision making model pushes people to deeper self-knowledge and indirectly to a deeper knowledge of our own culture, society or country.

The author proposes the development of a useful 3DEC to begin the process of testing and refining an approach that enables individuals to understand their own approach to ethical decisions making, in practice. The hopes are that it will enable someone to determine if their ethical decision making is consistent with their belief system.

6.0   Author's Bias Acknowledged

The author does not believe that morality or ethics can be relative to the situational context of the decision. Either an action is morally and ethically sound or it is not. As a result, the author believes that it is possible to create a scale that can be universally understood. The proposed 3DEC tool does not make a moral judgment as to the relative or absolute nature of one's ethical bias. It does create, however, a point for understanding, discussion and self-examination regarding the nature of one's 3DEC profile. As a result, the author sees the primacy of the ethics of the individual, and as secondary the overall ethical profile of any one group or organization. Why? Because the ethical profile of the group is a composite of the members of that group. If one wishes to change the ethical composition of the group, they must do it one 3DEC at a time.

7.0   Conclusion

In his evaluation and refinement of the Reidenbach and Robin study, Hansen (1992) writes that "While Reidenbach and

Robin (1990) have done a thorough job in analyzing the results from their research, the authors do not spend any time trying to link the results of their reduced multidimensional ethics scale to any ethical theory" (p. 533). In light of this critical examination of previous research in the field, it is important to note that a necessary component to a successful 3DEC would be a manner in which a 3DEC profile can be matched with an existing ethical theory. Further, it would be important to enable the interpreter of the 3DEC profile to ascertain whether the profile is consistent or inconsistent. Once tested, and refined, it should be possible to develop the 3DEC as a useful tool for a variety of applications.

A failure to have a consistent profile might be an indicator that the individual profiled has not spent enough time in critical examination of their decision making process. And this can be important to whom?

- Human resource managers determining who fits a company culture
- Managers seeking to promote individuals and need an understanding of how a candidate solves problems
- Individuals wanting to improve their ability to make decisions, or wanting to be more consistent in their successful problem solving
- Constituents wanting to understand how a candidate may approach legislation or decision making
- Anyone who wants to connect a decision making process to an ethical theory, whether in themselves or from someone else

Further, the author is in agreement with Friedman's assertion as follows:

Whether blameworthy or not, the use of the cloak of social responsibility, and the nonsense spoken in its name by influential and prestigious businessmen, does clearly harm the foundations of a free society. I have been impressed time and again by the schizophrenic character of many businessmen. They are capable of being extremely farsighted and clearheaded in matters that are internal to their businesses. They are incredibly shortsighted and muddleheaded in matters that are outside their businesses but affect the possible survival of business in general. This shortsightedness is strikingly exemplified in the calls from many businessmen for wage and price guidelines or controls or income policies. There is nothing that could do more in a brief period to destroy a market system and replace it by a centrally controlled system than effective governmental control of prices and wages. (para. 28)

In short, the effort to understand or elucidate one's ethical decision making process is very important. But, let us be certain that the effort does not end up reducing freedom, or making the exercise of one's individual's belief system prohibitive. The information gathered, and the comprehension gained, can be a starting point for increased understanding across national boundaries or cultural divides. But, it can also become the post upon which we pillory the failures of an individual for failing to meet an unexpressed cultural norm.

It is less important that corporations express satisfactory CSR, but it is of critical importance that executives, managers, and small business operators act in concert with a consistent, and thereby understandable ethical decision making process. One must not forget that decisions are made within the context of an individual, or group of individuals, understanding of what comprises right and wrong. At times, people make decisions to do wrong even though they know the decision is morally and ethically wrong.

An examination of the application of ethics in a business setting often fails to take into account the context of an individual's personal moral compass. People who are moral and ethical will make, in general, morally and ethically sound decisions. Those who do not have an anchored sense of right and wrong may or may not make ethically sound decisions.

It is not enough to call for and then improve ethical education in our business schools. It is not enough to create ethical position statements as corporations, whether large or small. It is not enough to call for the ethical investment and responsibility of large corporations to be enforced through government regulations, and that may be inappropriate. It is not enough to test the ethics of the masses in hopes of understanding better, how ethical decisions are being made. Until the application of "how" an individual makes ethical decisions, meets a clearly articulated "why" they need to make or should make those decisions, then a useful conversation regarding a practical ethic will not happen. The failure to do so will continually result in the relativistic morality of a few falling into ethical failures of epic proportions.

8.0   References

Alahmad, A. (2010). To be ethical or not to be: An international code of ethics for leadership. *Journal of Diversity Management, 5* (1), 31-35. http://search.proquest.com.proxy1.ncu.edu/docview/195579458?accountid=28180

Drucker, P. (1981). What is business ethics? *Public Interest, 63,* 18-36. Retrieved from http://www.nationalaffairs.com/doclib/20080708_1981632whatisbusinessethicspeterfdrucker.pdf

Friedman, M. (1970, September 13). The social responsibility of business to increase its profits. *New York Times,* New York , N.Y. 32-33, 122-124, 126. Retrieved from http://www.colorado.edu/studentgroups/libertarians/issues/friedman-soc-resp-business.html

Goss, B. (2010) Fundamental: Why churches and the Government can't solve our problems. *Unpublished manuscript.*

Hansen, R. S. (1992). A multidimensional scale for measuring business ethics: A purification and refinement. *Journal of Business Ethics, 11*(7), 523-523. Retrieved from http://search.proquest.com/docview/198023531?accountid=28180

Kemmerling, Garth. (27 October 2001). Socrates: Philosophical Life. *PhilosophyPages.Com.* Retrieved 23 October 2011. From http://www.philosophypages.com/hy/2d.htm

Murphy, P. (2009). The relevance of responsibility to ethical business decisions. *Journal of Business Ethics: Supplement, 90* 245-252. Retrieved from http://search.proquest.com.proxy1.ncu.edu/docview/365453640?accountid=28180

Schwartz, M. S., & Weber, J. (2006). A business ethics national index (BENI): Measuring business ethics activity around the world. *Business and Society, 45*(3), 382-382-405. Retrieved from http://search.proquest.com/docview/199399886?accountid=28180

What is DiSC®? (2010). Discprofile.com. Personality Profile Solutions, Inc. Retrieved 23 October 2011. Retrieved from http://www.discprofile.com/whatisdisc.htm

Proposing a Biblical Ethic for Environmentalism...

March 1st, 2007

If we can understand the genesis of the environmental movement, juxtapose the ideas and theories of environmentalism with the principles of Christianity then perhaps we can come to a more cogent understanding of how to approach a problem such as global warming. Additionally, there are other environmental concerns that are far easier to understand and accurately described such as Clean Air and Clean Water. That being said...

The green movement, "greenies", Earth First, Evangelical Christianity and the Environment, Green Peace, and Friends of the Earth are all names that are associated with a movement known as Environmentalism (Newton 139-144). As the name implies, this movement is concerned with the condition of our environment. However, the nature of the movement covers a broad spectrum of opinions regarding how the issue ought to be addressed. The issue is concerned with the necessity of protecting the environment from abuse. Whether one comes from the ultra-right or the radical left, the consensus is that there is a general problem in caring for our environment. Would you agree?

The current political approach in the United States today originates in the turbulent social upheavals of the early sixties (Kraft and Vig 9-10). However, the genesis of the movement can be traced back into the nineteenth century within the philosophy known as Romanticism. Loren Wilkinson explains:

For them [The Romantics], the proper use of the mind's distinctness from nature was the creative revitalization of the natural world. Coleridge's line, "in our life alone does Nature live," should not be read "without us nature is dead," but "with us nature *lives*. . . The imaginative synthesis of the mind with nature that, in light of the human imagination, now stood forth in a kind of radiant worth [which was] never before noticed (Earthkeeping 172).

The Romantic philosophy melded with the train of American thought and produced the Transcendentalists. The foremost spokesmen of this philosophy were Ralph Waldo Emerson and Henry David Thoreau. The impact of their thinking was most profound in that they stressed "a deep appreciation of the natural world and a fundamental critique of the manipulative attitude toward nature . . . " (Wilkinson, Earthkeeping, 173). This movement, along with the encouragement of John Muir and the Sierra Club, birthed the creation of national parks and the "forever wild" preserves (Wilkinson, Earthkeeping, 173-174).

By the beginning of the twentieth century, there were two basic views on nature: one which viewed nature as the repository of riches to be gathered and the other which viewed nature as needing preservation. Out of this deep tension between our need to use the land and our need to care for it emerged what today is commonly called the "environmental movement." In its first form it was primarily a concern for "conservation" . . . [On the heels of the disappearance of the frontier, there was] the beginning of that slow recognition of limitations on resources which in the last third of this century, has brought a model based on limits – the spaceship earth model – into the public consciousness (Wilkinson, Earthkeeping, 175).

The concept of the earth as a "spaceship" was shaped largely due to the influence of one man: Aldo Leopold. Leopold's understandings of the earth as the biosphere, a great network of living and nonliving things, has made us much more deeply aware of the land as not just "resources" but as our "environment." Thus, the environmental movement was born (Wilkinson, Earthkeeping, 177-179).

Politically speaking, the environmental movement did not find itself being reflected in policy until the 1970's. This decade saw a watershed in legislation dealing with the problem of preserving the environment. It also saw the creation of a federal organization: the Environmental Protection Agency (EPA). The basic trend of legislation during this time was directed toward the water, Clean Water Act (1970), and the air, Clean Air Act (1970), and avoided such issues as population growth and the energy crisis (Kraft and Vig 2-26). The question that still rages today is in what direction do we head now?

Should we mandate the Kyoto accords? Is there any credence to the Environmental Movement? Can it be approached from a biblical perspective? At its most basic level, it would seem that the controversy is whether the approach ought to be based upon "the concept of wise management and use of resources" or the "preservation of nature for its own sake" (Vig 53).

This is the crux of the matter for Christians in crafting a responsible approach to environmental concerns. If we are attempting not to trip, stumble, and maybe fall upon the sword of not caring, then how can we build an appropriate perspective on, or position the issue in the right venue for, the protection of the environment? How one views Nature and its purpose will largely determine the approach that one takes toward the movement in general. Due to the broad diversity of opinion on this issue, we will examine two separate approaches that define the broadest range of perspectives, and then suggest a balanced biblical orientation toward the environment.

The first approach concerns what is known as the Gaia Theory. This philosophical approach views the environment as an entity in and of itself. Todd Connor sums up this position: "The Gaia hypothesis is the scientific expression of the pre-Christian belief that the Earth is a living creature" (22). In other words:

. . . the idea is "that the earth's lower atmosphere is an internal, regulated, and necessary part of life itself, and that, for hundreds of millions of years, life has controlled the temperature, chemical composition, oxidizing ability, and acidity of the earth's atmosphere" (Connor 22).

The position when it was first proposed by James Lovelock was an attempt to explain the interrelatedness of life on the planet in a deeper, profound way, but without the religious overtones. The notion however, has carried over into the religious realm. Mr. Connor writes, "Gaia has a magical allure. It undermines biblical creation by imputing a kind of divine power to the Earth while offering a science that resonates with ancient mysticism" (25). Truly, the author of Ecclesiastes writes, "There is nothing new under the sun . . . " (Ecclesiastes 1:9). This approach is little more than the concept of a fertility goddess wrapped in the trappings of scientific theory.

James Lovelock, in cooperation with Lynn Margulis, has promoted the Gaia Theory on the grounds that the earth regulates itself. Lovelock states that "The biosphere is a self-regulating entity with the capacity to keep our planet healthy by controlling the chemical and physical environment" (Wilkinson

"Gaia Spirituality" 176). Lovelock is an atmospheric scientist, Margulis is a microbiologist, and neither views the theory in a religious light. The popular understanding of this theory, though, has had a theological impact on society. Why? "Gaia has irrevocably become part of the religious longings and language of our culture. This can be laid at the door of the second major reason for the spread of the Gaia idea: the desperate spiritual climate of our times" (Wilkinson "Gaia Spirituality" 180). The reaction of Margulis to this has been one of revulsion. She said in an interview in 1986 that the "religious overtones sicken me" (Connor 24).

The motivation of the preservation of the earth, in this model, is that the earth is a living entity that desires to be treated with respect. In fact, a geophysicist in San Francisco has suggested that Gaia "talks to herself:"

If we are "addicted, confused, and express disempowering tendencies, Gaia reacts with earthquakes, tornadoes, floods, and extreme weather changes that force us to reassess our values, work together, and create a way of life anew". . . And whenever "some conscious living entity" becomes enlightened about its true nature and its relationship to other living things, "Gaia is happy and experiences intrinsic joy herself" (Connor 25).

Not only does Gaia want to be treated with respect, but she "talks" to us as well. The result of this theology is the displacement of humanity from having a position of primacy in creation. Todd Connor quotes Ralph Metzner, an environmental activist in the following excerpt:

Humanity has a "reckless disregard for the delicately balanced interrelationships of the whole system" . . . The notion that human beings are intrinsically more valuable than a tree or a bug is now construed as a form of bigotry. Instead, all organisms are seen as vitally interrelated, and all plants and animals have the right to survive (25).

This view of the de-crowning of man as the pinnacle of creation is exhibited in some bizarre ways. For example, an extreme example of the logical thrust of both the theories of Evolution and of the Gaia are expressed in the Voluntary Human Extinction Movement (VHEMT), pronounced "Vehement," which suggest that the world really would be better off if humans voluntarily became extinct. On their website they state "When every human chooses to stop breeding, Earth's biosphere will be allowed to return to its former glory, and all remaining creatures will be free to live, die, evolve (if they believe in evolution), and will perhaps pass away, as so many of Nature's "experiments" have done throughout the eons."

Their website may be found at http://www.vhemt.org. There are wide ranges of topics discussed on their website, and some of them are definitely inappropriate for an immature or younger audience. But at this extreme end of the evolutionary-Gaia spectrum, we find people who have reduced humans to nothing more than an experiment of nature.

This approach finds its basis in the theory propagated by Lovelock and Margulis. This scientific theory, however, has also taken on religious overtones that seek to provide a motivation and ethical basis for the preservation of our environment. The approach combines aspects of the spiritual and the scientific.

The second approach to the Environment and its care finds its roots in a "frontier" mentality. Both David Newton and Loren Wilkinson define this viewpoint as seeing nature as a storehouse of "consumables" (Newton 25-36 and Wilkinson,

Earthkeeping, 162-169). This viewpoint has both an economic and religious basis that finds their wellspring in the early part of our nation's history. The English Colonies were viewed, by both the colonists and England, as a source of raw materials (Newton 27). "The dominant economic theme during the early years of the American nation was the utilization of natural resources" (Newton 27)

On the frontier, at least, nature was an enemy to be turned into a servant. There is little recorded to prove that the early settlers ever saw it as much more than that; they were merely trying to find a place to live and a source of food and pasture. The result was a great deal of practical knowledge about how to use the land, but not much interest in the land for its own sake (Wilkinson Earthkeeping 164).

In other words, the land had no intrinsic value in and of itself for the settlers. This attitude has translated to a view that sees nature as something to be conquered, something to be used, and not necessarily something that requires preservation.

The religious, or moral, aspect grew out of the Puritan ideals of hard work and the belief that the environment was to be subdued (Newton 35). Loren Wilkinson explains:

. . . something in the rigidity of the way God's relationship to his creatures was understood (though such an understanding was probably never Calvin's intention) seems to have entered the Protestant understanding of work – and hence, to have shaped our treatment of the earth . . . [There is] an assumption about the nature of dominion (God's dominion over us, our dominion over the earth) [which] has contributed to a harsh treatment of the earth, particularly in North America (Earthkeeping 168).

The Puritans believed that God has given man dominion over the earth, and therefore man is to subdue and rule the earth. This belief in conjunction with the "frontier mentality" towards the resources of the young American nation has resulted in the accusations made by Lynn White. "In 1967 historian Lynn White, in a widely publicized essay, faulted the church not only for its apathy, but for its contribution to environmental degradation. He charged that the theological concept of dominion was too easily cited to justify exploitation" (Frame 38). Loren Wilkinson wrote in Christianity Today:

That paper ("The Historical Roots of Our Ecological Crisis") [by Lynn White] called Christianity "the most anthropocentric religion the world has ever seen" and claimed that through such ideas as human dominion, the desacralizing of nature, and belief that the ultimate human destiny of is with God (and not the Earth) Christendom has encouraged a destructive use of creation ("Green Agenda" 16). This essay became the landmark work in criticizing the church, but toward evangelical protestants specifically, on their position concerning the environment (Wilkinson "Green Agenda" 16).

The primary factor in determining Christian's orientation to the environment has been the concept of dominion. This, along with the Christian's uneasiness with the more radical implications of the environmentalist movement's "neo-pagan bias," have been obstacles in constructing an evangelical position on the environment (Frame 39 and DeWitt 81-85).

Evangelical Christians, especially pre-millennialists, have been accused of not being concerned with the environment primarily because of their eschatology. This is clearly evidenced in the following assertion made by Al Truesdale:

So long as evangelicals hold to an eschatology that understands the world to exist under a divinely imposed death sentence, we should expect no major change in their disposition toward the environment or the environmental movement. They will continue to interpret environmental problems as among the first fruits of an imminent expression of divine wrath against "the late, great planet Earth." Invitations to participate in sustained efforts at solving environmental problems will be thought of as futile at best, and as defying God's will at worst (Truesdale 116).

This comprises what Truesdale has referred to as "an eschatology of despair." The question he raises is a legitimate one – can a premilliennialist espouse a concern for the environment that is consistent with his eschatological position? However, before examining the relevancy of the eschatological question, it will be helpful to examine some passages of scripture related to creation and how one ought to be disposed toward it. A key passage of scripture, some might posit *the* key passage, for examination and consideration is Genesis 1:26-28 (Bube 91):

Then God said, "Let us make man in Our image, after Our likeness; and let them have dominion over the fish of the sea, and over the birds of the air, over all the cattle, and over all the earth, and over every creeping thing that creeps upon the earth." ". . . And God blessed them, and God said to them, "Be fruitful and multiply, and fill the earth and subdue it; and have dominion over the fish of the sea and over the birds of the air and over every living thing that moves upon the earth."

In the past, the words *dominion* and *subdue* have been misconstrued as providing the justification for the exploitation of nature.

Most of the authors writing to define a Christian approach seek to describe a proper understanding of these words in light of the concept of stewardship. The Christian is to take care of the environment because of the divine command to take care of creation. Nowhere does Scripture promote the idea of oppressive domination; rather dominion and the command to subdue ought to be interpreted as referring to a "responsible stewardship" (DeWitt 84).

The overriding biblical principle that Christians ought to consider, in regards to environmentalism as a movement, is that of steward, or caretaker of the earth. Man ought to take care of what has been entrusted to him, because, ultimately, it is not his and the owner will eventually return to claim it as His own.

The issue or eschatology has been one that has led some to the position that nothing can be done to preserve or redeem creation. Those who follow the tradition of John N. Darby view the "conflagration" and the creation of the new heavens and the new earth as following the millennium (Bube 173-177). As a result, they see the ecological crisis as another indicator of the end times (Bube 173-177). In this view, only humans are ultimately saved and therefore resistance to environmental destruction is really a futile exercise (Wilkinson "Green Agenda" 20). Creation is viewed or understood to be *discontinuous*, in that the old earth and the old heavens will be destroyed at the end of time and recreated, or made anew.

There seems to be a general consensus among the authors who spoke about the eschatological issues on the *continuity* of creation. They are moving away from understanding the new heavens and the new earth as referring to a completely new creation. Rather, they view it as the "restoration of God's purposes" for creation. Or, as R.S. Beal Jr. writes ". . . at the return of Christ the earth will be renovated, restored, brought into a new and greater splendor (178). Chris Wright, in an article for Evangelical Review of Theology, quotes Frances Bridger on a proper impact of eschatology on a concern for the environment:

...the eschatological orientation of all biblical ethics has the important consequence of protecting our ecological concern from being either purely anthropocentric or pantheistically Earth-centered. The primary argument for ecological responsibility lies on the connection between the old and new creation. We are called to be stewards of the Earth by virtue of our orientation to the Edenic command of the Creator and also because of our orientation to the future. In acting to preserve and enhance the created, we are pointing to the coming of God in Christ. Ecological ethics are not, therefore, anthropocentric: they testify to the vindicating acts of god in creation and redemption. Paradoxically, the fact that it is God who will bring about a new order of creation at the end...need not act as a disincentive. Rather, it frees us from the burden of ethical and technological autonomy and makes it clear that human claims to sovereignty are relative. The knowledge that it is God's world... serves to humble us and bring us to the place of ethical obedience (166).

How then, can a Christian follow a biblically based ethic in caring for creation? Calvin De Witt, of the Au Sable Institute, lists the following principles that a steward of God's creation ought to consider following:

Biblical Principles for Creation Stewardship:

1. We must keep the creation as God keeps us.

2. We must be disciples of the Last Adam, not of the First Adam.

3. We must not press creation relentlessly, but must provide for its Sabbath Rests.

4. We may enjoy, but not destroy, the grace of God's good creation.

5. We must seek first the kingdom of God, not self-interest.

6. We must seek contentment as our great gain.

7. We must not fail to act on what we know is right.

Following the Creator, Sustainer and Reconciler of all creation is much more than reading – or even acting upon – these seven principles. But they can bring us more deeply into the scriptures and into contact with God's wider creation (140-143).

These principles allow the Christian to properly orient oneself to the environment. It is not necessary to see God as immanent, neither is necessary to devalue human life, nor to detract from man's position of primacy in creation, in order to value and care for the environment.

It is clear from the mountain of articles, books and pamphlets, that the environment is an issue that concerns many people. Scientists, theologians, housewives, and housewives, and teenagers, people from all walks of life are struggling to place themselves in a context with the environment. The issue strikes at both a religious orientation to life and at the proper view to take toward creation. It is possible to value nature, to see the environment as having intrinsic value, without making man an insignificant piece of it.

From Scripture, man has a mandate to care for the environment – in subduing and ruling the earth, he is not to destroy it for sordid gain, but to care for and preserve it. Praveen Kapur writes:

This Earth may be destroyed, but woe to us if we become the agents of destruction. Knowing that each one of us is ultimately going to die does not mean that we should not be taken care of, or that we should not care for ourselves. Even should the Earth one day come to an end, does nature also not have the right to be cared for and to live? Let there be life! (173)

For Christians, it is biblical both to be concerned about the environment and to be active in preserving it. As Loren Wilkinson writes, "Meeting human needs without a larger caring for the Earth is unbiblical and ultimately impossible" ("Green Agenda" 20).

As believers with a concern for the souls of men, it is imperative that we reach out to those who in their search for spiritual fulfillment have placed their faith in the worship of creation instead of the Creator. We need to demonstrate a real concern for our ecology and touch the souls that have become ensconced in the miry clay of Gaia.

People need the care of our heavenly Father and not the false sense of security that one might find in the reverence of Mother Nature. The environment can be evangelistic tool, instead of a religious turn-off. At an individual level, it is possible for the believer to rediscover the awe that is worthy only of a Mighty Creator. Philip Yance quotes from Ghillean Prance striking at the heart of a healthy view of the environment:

> *[Speaking of the experience of walking through a rain forest]* To begin with, it's wonderful that you can walk through it. The canopy cuts off nearly all sunlight, and in the shade, only a few low plants can grow. The forest is very still. In the canopy, you disturb the screeching birds and hear buzzing humming birds and howler

monkeys. You see tropical orchids – as many as 40 species of flowers in one treetop – and brilliantly colored frogs, butterflies, and beetles. In contrast, the forest floor is much more sedate.

If you keep very still, you may hear the chirping of katydids or cicadas. Lie down on the moist soil and you can see ten species of ants, and sometimes exotically camouflaged insects. Often you will hear the sudden roar of rain like a locomotive bearing down on you. At first you don't know the sound – you see, the forest canopy is so dense that it takes even the heaviest rain about ten minutes to filter through the vegetation. Then you'll feel the warm drops falling from the treetops 150 feet above.

To me, the only thing comparable is the experience of walking into one of the great cathedrals of England. You are awed, humbled, and stilled. You walk out purged by an almost sacred beauty, and when you leave, you are determined to defend that building, or that forest at any cost.[8]

---

[8] *Italics are mine*

References

Beal, R.S., Jr. "Can a Premillennialist Consistently Entertain a Concern for the Environment? A Rejoinder to Al Truesdale." Perspectives on Science and Christian Faith. 46 (1994): 173-178.

Bube, Richard H. "Do Biblical Models Need to Be Replaced In Order to Deal Effectively with Environmental Issues?" Perspectives on Science and Christian Faith. 46 (1994): 90-97.

Connor, Todd. "Is the Earth Alive?" Christianity Today. 11 January 1993: 22-25.

DeWitt,Calvin. "Christian Environmental Stewardship: Preparing the Way for action." Perspectives on Science and Christian Faith. 46 (1994): 80-89.

----."God's Love for the World and Creation's Environmental Challenge to Evangelical Christianity." Evangelical Review of Theology. 17(1993): 134-149.

Frame, Randy. "Christianity and Ecology: A Better Mix than Before." Christianity Today 23 April 1990: 38-39.

Huyser-Honig, Joan. "A Green Gathering of Evangelicals." Christianity Today. 5 October 1992: 56.

-----. "It's Not Easy Being Green." Christianity Today. 18 May 1992: 14.

Kapur, Praveen (Sunlil). "Let There Be Life: Theological Foundations for the Care and Keeping of Creation." Evangelical Review of Theology 17 (1993): 168-75.

Newton, David E. Taking A Stand Against Environmental Pollution. New York: Franklin Watts, 1990.

Nicholls, Bruce J. "Responding Biblically to Creation: A Creator-Centered Response to the Earth." Evangelical Review of Theology. 17 (1993): 209-222.

Sider, Ronald J. "Redeeming the Environmentalists." Christianity Today. 21 June 1993: 26-29.

Truesdale, Al. "Last Things First: The Impact of Eschatology on Ecology." Perspectives on Science and Christian Faith 41 (1994) 116-122.

Vig, Norman J. and Michael E. Kraft. "Environmental Policy from the Seventies to the Nineties: Continuity and Change" Environmental Policy in the 1990's. Washington D.C.: Congressional Quarterly Press, 1990.

Vig, Norman J. "Presidential Leadership: From Reagan to the Bush Administration." Environmental Policy in the 90's. Washington D.C.: Congressional Quarterly Press, 1990.

Wilkinson, Loren. Earthkeeping in the 90's: Stewardship of Creation. Grand Rapids: William B. Eerdmans Publishing Company, 1991.

---. "Gaia Spirituality: A Christian Critique." Evangelical Review of Theology. 17 (1993): 176-189.

---. "How Christian is the Green Agenda" Christianity Today. 11 January 1993: 16-20.

Yancey, Philip. "A Voice Crying Out in the Rain Forest." Christianity Today 22 July 1991: 26-28.

About the Author

Context is important. Here is a little bit of mine.

Benjamin is the oldest son of four, born in the early 1970's, which was a time of significant political and economic upheaval in the United States. After growing up in upstate New York and western Vermont, Benjamin left for college to attend Cairn University in Langhorne, PA (CairnU). While at CairnU, then known as Philadelphia College of Bible, he met his wife, Jenna Prather.

Benjamin and Jenna have lived in awesome cities across the United States including Philadelphia, Orlando, Phoenix, Denver, Kansas City and Omaha. Today, along with two Doberman Pinschers named Penelope and Roxie, a Pembroke Welsh Corgi named Lilly, and one hamster named Liberty, they are raising five incredibly active and intelligent children, 3 boys and 2 girls, who range in age from 6 years to 18 years.

Benjamin and Jenna are active in their community and in their church, online, musically and in service. Their children have participated in activities ranging from music lessons, to gymnastics, to the Boy Scouts of America & Heritage Girls. They believe strongly in the value of education. Jenna teaches the children at home and is working on her MBA.

Benjamin finished his MBA at Regis University in Denver, Colorado. He is taking a break from pursuing a Doctorate in Business Administration. He holds degrees in Religion, Education, History, and Business.

www.ingramcontent.com/pod-product-compliance
Lightning Source LLC
Chambersburg PA
CBHW060839280326
41934CB00007B/843